Rc

CW01669311

GOVERNING BODIES OF THE MNAC
Generalitat de Catalunya
Ajuntament de Barcelona

PRESIDENT
Joan Guitart i Agell

VICE-PRESIDENT
Joan Majó i Cruzate

MEMBERS
Josep Anton Acebillo i Marín
Lluís Domènech i Girbau
Joan Fuster i Sobrepere
Josep M. Huguet i Reverter
Ferran Mascarell i Canalda
Joaquim de Nadal i Caparà
Antoni Pladevall i Font
Manuel Ribas i Piera
Aurora Sanz i Manrique
Josep Serra i Solans
Francesc Vicens i Giralt

SECRETARY
Antoni Balari i Zanotti

DIRECTOR
Eduard Carbonell i Esteller

CHIEF ADMINISTRATOR
Ramon Fort i Marrugat

SPONSORS
Banco Central Hispano
Bassat, Ogilvy & Mather
Fomento de Construcciones y Contratas, S.A.
Freixenet, S.A.
Gallina Blanca
Gas Natural SDG
SEAT
Ràdio-Televisió Espanyola de Catalunya
Televisió de Catalunya, S.A.
Winterthur

Romanesque art guide

MNAC
MUSEU NACIONAL D'ART DE CATALUNYA

AUTHORS

Eduard Carbonell i Esteller
Director

Montserrat Pagès i Paretas
Curator of the Romanesque Art Department

Jordi Camps i Sòria
Curator of the Romanesque Art Department

Teresa Marot
Curator of the Numismatic Collection

General Assistant : Mercè Saura

DOCUMENTATION

Biblioteca General d'Història de l'Art
Department of Documentation and Registration of artworks
Conservation Department

EDITION AND PRODUCTION

Publications Department
Núria Giralt
Gemma Ylla-Català

Collaborators on the translation,
Paul Hammond and Elena Llorens

PHOTOGRAPHS

The Photograpgic Service
Jordi Calveras, Marta Mèrida and Joan Sagristà

GRAPHIC DESIGN

Claret Serrahima i associats: Irene Ferrer-Mayol

COLOUR SEPARATIONS AND FILMS

Retoscan, S.A.

PRINTING

Grup 3

©Edition
Museu Nacional d'Art de Catalunya
Palau Nacional, Parc de Montjuïc
08038 Barcelona

©Texts and photographs : Museu Nacional d'Art de Catalunya

First edition: 1998
Second edition: 2000
ISBN : 84-8043-039-7
Legal deposit : B-46.060-98

Contents

Introduction

The history of the Museum's Romanesque art collection

THE INSTALLATION OF the Romanesque art collections in the Palau Nacional de Montjuïc goes back to the 1930s. The Museu d'Art de Catalunya was created at that time as part of a general reorganisation of museum policy, and was opened to the public in 1934. The Palau Nacional, built as the symbol of the 1929 International Exposition, has since that date housed the collections of Catalan art. At that time the Museum already possessed the greater part of its Romanesque art collection, although notable collections and individual works of art would go on being added to it.

The gradual formation of the Romanesque art collection often has much to do with the cultural programmes initiated by Catalan institutions and by civil society itself, a factor which did not occur with the collections of other institutions. One must also acknowledge private iniciative, and its desire to safeguard and publicise the cultural and artistic heritage of Catalonia, through art collectors and their donations and legacies to public institutions. On the whole, both collective and individual efforts —at times symbolised by exceptional personalities— have been decisive factors in the shaping of the Romanesque art collection, and the Museum as a whole.

With the passing of the 1990 Llei de Museus (law relating to the organisation of the country's museums) approved by the Catalan Parliament, the Museu Nacional d'Art de Catalunya (MNAC) was created, with the aim of furthering to the historical goals of the Museum. As a result, the new Romanesque exhibition gallery was opened in December 1995. However, the long road towards achieving these aims must be mapped out as it is obviously interwoven with the history of the Museum and the study of Romanesque and medieval art in Catalonia.

The awakening of interest in Romanesque art. The first collections

The antecedents of the Museum go back to the 19th century, to a series of interventions aimed at safeguarding and promoting Catalan artistic and archaeological heritage which was in danger of being dispersed, or of vanishing altogether. Let us recall, for example, the abandonment and destruction of numerous religious buildings as the result of events such as the 1836 disentailment. This led to the formation of a small museum of antiquites which was administered by the Reial Acadèmia de Bones Lletres and situated in the old convent of Sant Joan de Jerusalem in Barcelona, no longer extant today. A few stone artefacts that today form a part of the Romanesque art collection come from that museum.

Interest in the medieval world gradually began to emerge, linked to the spirit of Romanticism as it was manifested in other European countries. In Catalonia, this awakening of interest coincided with the wish to know more about the country itself, to define and claim a particular identity. As a result, medieval art was subject to revalorization, supported by new scientific methodologies.

Within this context, interest in Romanesque panel painting went on developing, especially as a result of the exhibitions held in Barcelona and in Vic in 1867 and 1868, and a short time later, at the Universal Exposition of Barcelona in 1888. The diocese of Vic lent a series of Romanesque altar frontals to be shown at the latter. Also exhibited was a frontal from the Barnola Collection (later called from Esquius) which decades later was entrusted to the Museum of Barcelona.

In this process of recovery and study of art and archaeology in Catalonia, the city of Vic —where the Museu Episcopal was founded in 1891— acquired a special prominence. In 1896 the Museum of Solsona was created. In Barcelona, the first important collection of Romanesque art —which is now associated with the MNAC— had previously formed a part of the Museo Provincial de Antigüedades in Barcelona and the Museu Municipal de Belles Arts. The former, opened in 1880 in the chapel of Santa Àgata, contained chiefly objects made of stone that came, in part, from the collection of the Reial Acadèmia de Bones Lletres. The latter was installed in 1891 in the Palau de Belles Arts, built for the 1888 Universal Exposition of Barcelona, and housed some of the most outstanding panel paintings of the current collection. One of these was the *Frontal from Ix* (Hix, Cerdagne), which was added to the Museum's collection in 1889.

During that time, there had also been a reorganization of the commission in charge of museums, and in 1902 it became the Board of Museums and Fine Arts (Junta Municipal de Museus i de Belles Arts). That same year, the new board organised the *Exhibition of Ancient Art*, which contained a selection of works from the artistic heritage of Catalonia. The Board of Museums was essential in defining the parameters of the Romanesque art collection. One of the members of the board was especially active: Josep Pijoan, who in 1906 led an expedition to La Seu d'Urgell and La Cerdanya that would result in new acquisitions. The collection was thus enriched by works in other media, such as sculpture *(The Christ from 1147)* and enamelling *(Incense boat from Ars)*.

Discovery and study of Romanesque murals

A key year in the history of the Museum was 1907. Until then, only a few researchers had devoted themselves to the study of murals: among them were Josep Puiggarí, author of the first serious study on the known paintings from Sant Quirze in Pedret, and Jean-Auguste Brutails, who had published a study on the paintings of Sant Martí de Fenollar (Saint-Martin de Fenouillar) in the region of Vallespir.

Due to the initiative of Enric Prat de la Riba, the Institut d'Estudis Catalans was set up in 1907, whose members included notable personalities such as Josep Pijoan and Josep Puig i Cadafalch, who decided to focus his research on Romanesque architecture. That same year, the Institute organized the 'Official Archaeological Mission to the Aragon Border', mainly to the upper Ribagorça area. During this expedition, the churches of Taüll and Boí and in particular their frescoes came to light.

About the same time, paintings had also begun to be discovered in other areas of the Pyrenees, and in regions such as Osona and Vallès. The Junta de Museus (Board of Museums), which had been reorganised in 1907, decided to commission copies of the frescoes that had been discovered or were being studied, using a procedure adopted in France a few years earlier. These copies would later be published in the book *Les Pintures Murals Catalanes* (Catalan Mural Paintings) by Josep Pijoan, and they also bore witness to the desire to conserve some record of the originals given the precarious state of preservation of both the paintings and the churches.

All these initiatives can be situated within the context of *Noucentisme* (a cultural and political movement born in Catalonia at the beginning of the 20th century) of which Josep Pijoan is considered one of the most representative exponents, as well as being the inspirer of a number of cultural projects of the time.

Romanesque art in la Ciutadella. The installation of the murals

As a consequence of museum policies which began to go into effect at the beginning of the century, the Museu de Belles Arts moved to the former la Ciutadella arsenal in 1915. It should be noted that these changes took place within the political framework of the Mancomunitat de Catalunya, established in 1914 and presided over by Enric Prat de la Riba. Among the new additions to the collection, the then Museu d'Art i Arqueologia included another of the major pieces in the current collection, *The Batlló Majesty.*

Interest in Romanesque murals deepened considerably, embracing the world of art commerce as well. These circumstances motivated an attempt to export a number of works, in an operation calling on Italian technical expertise to remove the frescoes from the wall. The Board of Museums, which included Joaquim Folch i Torres —who had been director of the Museum's Section of Medieval and Modern Art since 1918— reacted in time and brought the operation to a halt, but the paintings from the central apse of the church in Mur finally left the country to go to the Museum of Fine Arts in Boston. After an internal debate at the Board of Museums, it was decided that the paintings would be moved to Barcelona and installed in the Museum. This operation was carried out between 1919 and 1923. The process and the details of the entire operation of the removal, transportation and installation of the paintings constitutes an important moment in the history of the Museum which has been well documented and thoroughly explained on many occasions.

Installation of the paintings from Sant Climent (Taüll) in the Museu d'Art i Arqueologia (1924).

Folch i Torres, director of the Museum after 1920, was to be one of the most important names in the history of the Museum and the Romanesque art collection. Under his supervision, the exhibition rooms of the la Ciutadella were remodelled to display the mural collections which for the most part came from the apses of remote churches. Among these groups, the ones from Santa Maria in Taüll, Sant Joan in Boí and Sant Pere in La Seu d'Urgell stood out, and of course the apse from Sant Climent in Taüll —which from that time on was to become the most paradigmatic image in the Museum's Romanesque art collection. The new installation was inaugurated in 1924, and the Romanesque art section has been known since then by the singularity of its frescoes.

Romanesque art on Montjuïc. New contributions to the Romanesque art collection

In the 1930's, another decisive moment in the history of the Museum took place. As we have remarked before, in 1934 the Museu d'Art de Catalunya was opened to the public in the Palau Nacional on Montjuïc. This building, which had earlier housed the exhibition *Art in Spain* in 1929, would provide a more suitable space for the display of the mural groups due in large part to the height of its ceilings.

Previously, in 1932, the Romanesque collection had been considerably enlarged by the acquisition of the Plandiura Collection. Apart from the new group of murals, the number of objects employing diverse artistic techniques was increased, particularly with metalwork and enamelling.

However, when the Spanish Civil War (1936-1939) broke out, the resulting danger to the collection prompted measures directed towards safeguarding the works of art in the Palau Nacional. To protect them, they were moved to Olot and to locations in the Pyrenees. In Paris in 1937, an exhibition of Catalan art was organised in the Jeu de Paume, which was later shown in the Château de Maisons-Laffitte, and included works from the Museum, some of which were Romanesque, thus contributing to their becoming known abroad. After the end of the war, —and the change in the political situation— the Romanesque art section was installed in the Palau Nacional in 1942.

Installation of the paintings from Santa Maria (Taüll) in the Museu d'Art de Catalunya (1934).

The display in the rooms 12 and 14 (Sant Climent in Taüll) in the Museu d'Art de Catalunya (1973).

Since then, the Museum collection has continued to be enlarged by private contributions, the arrival of the Espona bequest in 1958 being particularly significant among other new additions to the mural collection which continued until the 1970s under the direction of Joan Ainaud de Lasarte. The importance of the Romanesque art collection was evident to everyone at the international exhibit *Romanesque Art,* which was organized in 1961 under the auspices of the Council of Europe, being held in both Barcelona and Santiago de Compostela. The Museum exhibition rooms were especially prepared to accommodate the show.

Years later, the Romanesque section was remodelled and inaugurated in 1973 with the incorporation in the permanent exhibition room of recent mural acquisitions and a revised presentation of many of the groups. In 1987, a few exhibition rooms were closed off, but most areas of the Museum stayed open to the public until the summer of 1990 when its doors were closed to prepare for another remodelling. During the time the Museum was closed, pieces from the medieval art collection were part of exhibitions both in Catalonia and elsewhere. Finally, and as has already been mentioned, in December 1995 the new Romanesque exhibition rooms of the MNAC were inaugurated.

Mural painting and the technique for removing it

MURAL PAINTING FORMS the most important part of the Romanesque art collection. The Museum possesses and exhibits a great many mural groups, most of them having a religious subject matter. They mainly come from different areas of Catalonia, but most of all from churches in the Boí Valley: for example the famous paintings of Sant Climent in Taüll, the most representative work in the collection; the major group from Santa Maria in Taüll; and the one from the church of Sant Joan in Boí, partially reassembled recently. Another striking ensemble is the one attributed to the Pedret Circle, made up of stylistically very similar paintings (Pedret, Àneu, El Burgal, etc.). Moreover, pictorial groups from other former Iberian kingdoms are displayed. These are not church decorations, but come from monastic buildings, such as the magnificent chapter house group from the Aragonese nunnery of Santa María in Sigena, saved after a fire which took place during the Spanish Civil War, and the palatine hall group from the Castilian monastery of San Pedro in Arlanza, decorated with frescoes of secular and mythological subject matter.

Most of the buildings where these paintings originally came from are still standing and in use. Some of them have been restored and others are in the process of being restored, as in the case of the church of the monastery of Sant Pere in El Burgal, or the still impressive monumental group from San Pedro in Arlanza (Burgos). The major part of the paintings exhibited in the Museum was acquired by the Board of Museums between 1919 and 1923, in a campaign that attempted to save the mural paintings from being exported and to assure that they stayed in the country. The decision to carry out this campaign was taken after discovering that the Romanesque paintings from the main apse of Santa Maria in Mur had been sold to foreign antique dealers. When the Board of Museums acquired the paintings, they also ordered their removal and transfer, which was carried out by the Italian Franco Steffanoni from Bergamo in Lombardy, assisted by Arturo Dalmati and Arturo Cividini.

Romanesque wall painting was executed using the fresco technique, which consists of applying pigments diluted in limewater while the plaster on the wall is still fresh, or damp. When the painting dries, the lime crystallizes so that the painting becomes fused to the wall. Nevertheless, for reasons of conservation and protection, the frescoes can be removed from the wall, a procedure that has been practised in Italy since ancient times. Basically, the operation consists of removing the paintings from their original support, the wall, and transferring them to a second, canvas. To do this with the utmost guarantee of success, the pictorial layer must first be consolidated and protected. The next step consists of placing two consecutive layers of cotton cloth, the removal canvas, spread with organic glue, to the paintings so that they remain firmly affixed for later removal. When these layers have firmly adhered to the paintings, the latter can be removed from the wall by using either the *strappo* or the *stacco* technique. The *strappo* technique pulls away only the pictorial layer, without the mortar. When the *stacco* technique is used, the preparatory mortar comes off with the pictorical layer. The use of one procedure or another depends on the state of preservation of the paintings to be removed. Most of the paintings in the Romanesque exhibition hall were removed from the wall by the *strappo* technique. Once they are removed, the paintings are transferred to a canvas by means of lime casein. Then, after the paintings are transferred to the new support, the removal canvas can be eliminated. Finally the paintings are put on stretchers, which may be flat, or they may reproduce the architecture on which the mural originally reposed, as in most of the groups on show in the Museum.

Removal of the paintings from Santa Maria in Taüll (1922).

The museological and the museographical project

THE MUSEOLOGICAL DISCOURSE of a museum is conditioned by the collection of works that it houses. The quality, variety and number of works conserved in a given museum will inevitably determine said discourse.

Secondly, this discourse, in the case of the Museu Nacional d'Art de Catalunya, is also determined by the Llei de Museus passed by the Catalan Parliament in November 1990. According to this law, the MNAC must explain the history of Catalan art in relation to the art of its neighbours and, whenever it is possible, to that of the international sphere.

These two factors have in part determined the museological discourse when it came time to plan the permanent exhibition of Romanesque art. However, the second factor can itself be understood as a description of the Museum collection, primarily from Catalonia and its neighbours. In that sense, the discourse has been determined by the existing collections.

As a consequence, four premises have defined *a priori* the development of the museological discourse. In the first place, an understanding of art as something that changes through time; yet also to conceive of the classification of styles, which doubtless exist, as a means of identifying works according to formal characters which correspond to the general viewpoint of a period, both for the artist and spectator. Iconography also plays an essential role in this development, since new themes continue to be incorporated in accordance with the changing ways of thinking at any one historical moment. Thus, art conforms to a constant process of development and change, and the defining features of diverse styles often coexist in a work of art. Beyond the concepts of Romanesque, Gothic, Renaissance and so forth, our ambition would be to make this sense of continuity prevail, namely that art changes along with time. It is in this respect that the starting point of our discourse engages with the tradition of sculpture prior to the Romanesque age.

The second premise consists of offering an overall picture of the art of an age, in accordance with the availability of the collections, and bearing in mind the specialisations of other museums in the city of Barcelona where other arts and artistic media are considered: in other words, this is an attempt to consider all the artistic media —sculpture, painting, drawing, applied arts— and their development over the course of time. The MNAC is not only a museum of painting and sculpture, but rather a museum which can and should offer an overview of art from the Romanesque period to the first half of the 20th century.

Dismounting and removal of the apse from Santa Maria d'Àneu prior to its new, 1995 installation.

The third premise leads us to the enrichment through parallel and specific readings, of the chronological and stylistic discourse which forms the connecting of the exhibition. When the collection renders this possible, by making a diachronic halt certain aspects of the art and the period are highlighted which enhance the spectator's greater understanding. This may mean iconographic subject matter, the evolution of particular forms and styles, or aspects relating to technique or to society.

Retouching of the paintings from Sant Joan in Boí prior to their new, 1995 installation.

The fourth premise is determined by the essence of the Museum, which is an art and not a history museum. Our major concern has been to safeguard the direct relationship between the spectator and the work of art. We have strived to maintain a relationship largely based on the contemplation of the works on display, leaving to one side, and in parallel, all those elements which help to contextualise the work from a historical point of view. The explanatory information is made up of the texts displayed in each section, the explanatory showcases, the accompanying brochure and the video.

In the first section, three tombstones with their corresponding inscriptions in Latin, Arabic, and Hebrew, facilitate the visitor's introduction to the historical and social context of the age, and point to the presence of different, interfacing cultures which coexist within the developmental framework of Romanesque art. A showcase, with coins used when the area was ruled by counts marks the chronological beginnings of the period. Such links with history will be displayed in other numismatic showcases throughout the exhibit.

Presiding over this first section, we find the apse of Sant Pere in La Seu d'Urgell, a magnificent work that exemplifies the most characteristic part of the collection: Romanesque mural painting.

From this first section on, it is such apses —which are placed in chronological and stylistic order— which form the thread of the tour through the Romanesque exhibition. The works of art which employ other artistic techniques follow the same discourse, and are placed around the focal point of the mural paintings.

Thus, the museological project is basically chronological and stylistic. The diverse artistic techniques illustrate stylistic development throughout the course of time. The changes that gradually occurred in the development of Romanesque art —especially in Catalonia— are illustrated by the works in the collection. This stylistic development took place from the 11th to the 13th century.

On this tour, the chronological and stylistic discourse is enriched by specific sections which allow us to explain technical, formal and iconographic aspects of Romanesque art. Moreover, from time to time, a particular historical or sociological aspect is illustrated by a specific artwork. These sections allow the visitor to deepen his or her knowledge of Romanesque art by recourse to other possible readings.

For instance, works of art are analysed and compared from a technical viewpoint —as in the case of the altar frontals and their relationship to gold and silverwork. Or indeed the formal development of the earliest architectural sculpture is presented, establishing a relationship with 10th-century Islamic works. Through iconographic analysis the most characteristic typologies and images of an eminently religious art such as the Romanesque are explained; in this instance the iconography of Christ and the Virgin. In these sections, the works illustrating such themes are grouped independently of general chronological discourse, given that the idea is to show the typology, variants, and development of an iconographic subject matter. Within this iconographic sphere, some sections have only one work for illustrating the subject of angels or saints.

Likewise, an attempt has been made to explain certain historical concepts: like for instance, the extent of episcopal power, and to illustrate this through enamelling, plus coins minted by the bishops themselves.

The objective is, therefore, to enrich the vision of Romanesque art by appealing to as many readings as possible, using the Museum collection as a starting point. However, these readings can only be undertaken when the artworks permit it. As always, any museological discourse is conditioned by the collection itself.

The museographical project

The museological project conditions the museographical project. The space dedicated to the permanent exhibition of the Romanesque art collection is also fundamentally determined by the 1929 building itself which limits the museographical discourse. The plans of the architects Gae Aulenti and Enric Steegmann have respected the architecture of the building.

But what defines the museographical project is, without doubt, the presence of the mural paintings, the apses and the other architectural aprioris that give the Museum its unique character, with regard to the Romanesque art collections and their display, in other words, its museography.

The architectural groups of mural painting dictate the visitors' tour. But their display has been planned with two distinct concepts in mind. Firstly, the apses are defined as museographical objects in themselves, which means that they are seen without any attempt at concealing what supports the mural paintings:

that is to say, the backs of the apses are in full view. Secondly, in six particular instances the pictorial groups are included in rooms of larger dimensions which can reproduce or at least evoke at a scale of 1:1, albeit in a fragmentary manner, the actual space from whence the paintings came; this is the case of the lateral aisles from Sant Joan in Boí, the churches of Sant Climent and Santa Maria in Taüll, the nave from Sant Pere in Sorpe, the atrium from Sant Vicenç in Cardona and the chapter house from the Aragonese nunnery of Santa María in Sigena.

A number of white walls determine the route between the apses. There is one route, and one route alone. It is on these white walls, and sometimes in the showcases, that different examples of architectural sculpture, religious imagery, panel paintings, enamelwork and coins are exhibited.

Lighting is essential to the spatial layout. Light is projected directly onto the pieces, without recourse to ambient light, so that the artworks are partly immersed in shadow. The apse paintings are lit from below.

Throughout the tour, the didactic aids are twofold: firstly, the presentation texts and brief explanations of each one of the twenty-one sections, and secondly, the showcases provide information on the main mural groups, thus encouraging greater understanding on the part of the visitor. There is also supplementary material available about the exhibition: audiovisual material, didactic guidebooks, and so forth.

Instructions for using the guide

The texts that refer to the Romanesque Gallery and to the works of art are organised in the following manner: each section has an ample introduction that provides a commentary for each and every one of the works displayed in relation to the museographical discourse. Following these introductions there are a series of entries which contain explanations of the works selected according to their importance or representative nature. These are the pieces cited in the introductions to the section followed by a highlighted number (for example: *Apse from Sant Pere in La Seu d'Urgell,* **1**). In the sections which have only one work of art, or one mural group, the explanatory comments are included in the introductory text of the section in which it appears. Some mural groups are explained at length, because of their simbolic character or their determining function in the museographical project, since they have defined the order in which the works are presented in the Romanesque Gallery. That is why in some cases the floor plans of the churches where the paintings come from are shown, indicating the original siting of the paintings before being removed from the wall and transferred to the Museum.
Both the introductions of the sections and the explanations of the works include references to other works, whether or not they belong to the Museum, for reasons of comparison. If the works are exhibited, their section number is indicated in Roman numerals, and their number within the particular room in Arabic numbers. For example: *Voussoir from Ripoll* (VI, 84).
At the end of the guide there is a list of all the works exhibited and their technical specifications, including those for which a commentary was not supplied.
After the list, a bibliography and a glossary of useful terms will be found.

SECTION I

Introduction. The apse paintings from Sant Pere in La Seu d'Urgell

A VISIT TO the permanent exhibition of the Romanesque art collection begins with two important features which help to situate a period in Catalan history and the beginning of an age, the age of Romanesque art. Firstly, three tombstones reveal the presence of three different cultures during the Middle Ages: the first tombstone has a Latin inscription in uncial and capital letters (11); the second, with an Arabic inscription in Kufic script (10); and the third, with a Hebrew inscription (12). Secondly, the chronological parameters are defined in a showcase **9** where a collection of the most representative coins of the 'Marca Hispanica' territory is assembled, starting from the Carolingian age to the days of Count Ramon Berenguer I (1035-1076). The historical reference point indicated by the coinage remains evident throughout the exhibition, which ends at the showcase that contains the royal money from the reign of James I, the Conqueror (XVIII, 146).

Following this contextualising note on the history of the country, the mural group from the *Apse from Sant Pere in La Seu d'Urgell* **1** presides over this section. This opus has been chosen for its monumentality, as a paradigm of the twenty-six Romanesque mural groups that can be seen in the Museum, and because it introduces a subject frequently depicted on apse vaulting: a Theophany, a vision or apparition of Christ in His Glory (*Maiestas Domini*). In this case, it depicts the Second Coming of Christ on the Day of Judgement. The literary sources are from Revelations; the visions of Isaiah, Ezekiel and Daniel —all relating to the Last Judgement, and the advent of the Kingdom of God. The iconographic origins of this type of Theophany are to be found in Christian art of the late Roman period; later these representations were influenced by Carolingian art and by the art of Byzantium, up until their formulation as Romanesque art. In the specific case of Catalan Romanesque art, the iconographic models reached Catalonia by different routes, in particular from the regions of central and southern France, and the north of

Italy. Returning to the *Apse from Sant Pere in La Seu d'Urgell,* the portrayal of the *Maiestas Domini* is surrounded by the depiction of the Tetramorph, the symbols of the Four Evangelists according to St. Jerome: the lion for Mark, the angel for Matthew, the ox for Luke and the eagle for John.

The *Altar from Sant Serni de Tavèrnoles* **2** has been placed within the apse. This is due to its monumentality, apart from the original proximity to the altar and to the paintings in the Church of Sant Pere in La Seu d'Urgell. The painting treats an infrequently seen iconographic subject in Catalan Romanesque panel painting: the potential exaltation of St. Sernin, Bishop of Toulouse, Languedoc.

Because of certain formal and stylistic features, historiography has linked the *Frontal from La Seu d'Urgell* **3** and the *Frontal from Ix* (Hix, Cerdagne) (4) to the murals in La Seu d'Urgell. The first, which shows the figure of the *Maiestas Domini* in the centre of a double mandorla (a frequent characteristic of models with Carolingian roots), presents, to eitherside, two groups each with six apostles in a perfectly symmetrical spatial configuration. The *Frontal* *from Ix* (4) has the same central design and a close stylistic resemblance, containing scenes dedicated to St. Martin, along with the apostles. Certain stylistic and iconographic aspects indicate that these works may be related to the miniature.

In this first section, in addition to the mural and panel painting, there are also samples of other Romanesque artistic techniques: stonework, wood carving and metalwork. Stonework is represented by a small pre-Romanesque altar, later used as a holy water stoup (5). As for wood carving, the 13th-century *Cubells Christ* (6) is shown, with its complex iconography with features of a suffering Christ (*patiens*) and wearing a triumphal crown; in addition the figure of the Holy Virgin, the image most often seen in this type of carving, is represented here by the *Pruneres Virgin* (7). Lastly, the technique of gilded and chiselled bronze is represented by the figure of the *Moror Christ* (8) which dates from *c.* 1180.

Since the collections permit it, this first section tackles the subject of the formal development of stone sculpture from the 6th century to the

32 *Coinage of the Counts and Bishops*

32.5

AT THE END OF THE 10th century and throughout the 11th, the progressive weakening of Carolingian power enabled the most influential Catalan counts to take over the rights to mint their own money as a symbol of power and sovereignty, and as a royal prerogative. (32.1 & 32.2). The Counts of Barcelona, who had gradually achieved supremacy over the other Catalan counts, granted part of the rights to mint money, and the ensuing profits, to the Bishops of Osona (Vic) and later to the Counts of Girona, who struck *diners* and obols of great artistic and technical quality (32.4, 32.5 & 32.6).

In this historical context, splendid coins were minted. They are distinguished by their typological richness and variety of their religious subject matter and by their technical quality, adapting the chosen figures with great boldness on metal of reduced size. The depictions of angels and saints (32.8) and of prominent people shown in an attitude of blessing, demonstrate the influence that episcopal power exercised in the minting of coins. At the same time, motifs of obvious Byzantine origin were depicted; these were seldom seen on Christian coins in the West, for example the effigy of Christ crowned with a cruciferous nimbus on the coins of Girona and the image of a veiled Mary on the coins from Besalú (32.3) and Girona (32.7).

Romanesque period in order to demonstrate the evolution of this artistic technique. It contains pieces that proceed from Islamic and Christian monuments dating from the early Middle Ages. The first two specimens belong to the age of Visigothic rule and reflect the continuity of the late Roman Empire in the use of bevelled carving **(13)** and Corinthian capitals **(14)**. The next pieces display the richness and creativity of Al-Andalus art in Cordoba and the surrounding area, especially during the Caliphate **(15-19)**. The other capital **(20)**, which is included in the category that historiography defines as a 'Caliphal type', reflects the possible influence of Caliphal art on certain Catalan Christian artefacts during the 10th century. In any case, this example constitutes a some what rustic version when compared to others that are more representative, for example those in Ripoll and Cornellà de Llobregat. An Islamic piece from the 11th century can be seen: it is a figurative plaque **(21)** from Toledo, that dates from the time of the kingdoms of *Taifas*. At its side, there are fragments from the Barcelona Cathedral **22** and from Sant Pere in Àger **(23)**. They are examples from a limited sculptural repertory of simple plant and geometric forms (palmettes, interlacing, etc.) in bevelled relief. This sculpture is almost contemporaneous with the first attempts at decorating façades using figuration, as in the examples of Sant Genís de Fontanes (Saint-Génis-des-Fontaines) and Sant Andreu de Sureda (Saint-André-de-Sorède) in Roussillon. Lastly, we see artefacts related technically to 11th-century works, and also to those from the 12th century in their structure and their decorative repertory **(24 & 25)**.

After this synthetic overview of Romanesque art exhibited in this first section, which incorporates the formal development of sculpture, we now begin a chronological tour of the gallery.

1 *Apse from Sant Pere in La Seu d'Urgell*

FIRST HALF OF THE 12th CENTURY

THE APSE COMES FROM the Church of Sant Pere (today Sant Miquel i Sant Pere), in the cathedral group of La Seu d'Urgell. Although the Theophany on the vaulting portrays the most characteristic iconographic subject in this part of the Romanesque building (see the introduction to this section), it presents some special features. The *Maiestas Domini* (Christ in Majesty) is shown in all His glory within the mandorla, surrounded by the Tetramorph which is only partially preserved. However, the height of the figure, the folds of the drapery, the position of the feet and the lack of a seat of honour would indicate that Christ is standing, as in some very early Christian examples. Some authors have interpreted this as an evocation of the Ascension, as on the façade of the Cathedral in Angoulême, Charente. Nevertheless, there are a few iconographic elements on the *Apse of Sant Pere in La Seu d'Urgell* which allow the subject matter to be identified as the Second Coming of Christ, His triumphal return at Doomsday to judge the living and the dead. Firstly, because the figure is giving a blessing with his right hand and holds a book in his left;

and on the other hand, the remains of an inscription (' [...] *DO QVAE SVMPSI MEMBRA VEHENDO'* and '[...] *NDE RECRE* [...] *IVDEX SAN* [...]'), from some *carmina* or liturgical chants on the vision and the Last Judgement, reinforce this identification.

The Apostles and the Virgin are shown grouped in pairs on the semicircular part of the apse, below a splendid border and the inscription quoted above. Andrew and Peter proffer their emblems, the cross and the keys, and Mary, who is next to John the Evangelist, holds a crown in a draped hand, which may be an allusion to her position as the Queen of Heaven, praised in the litanies. We can recognize Paul in the couple further to the right.

The flowing style, the sureness of line in the paintings, and the tendency toward a geometricisation of the drapery have been linked to the classically oriented, monumental aesthetics of the Provençal school of sculpture, while the whitewashed background —where the figures on the vaulting are depicted— has been linked to pictorial examples from Occitania and central France. The nearest stylistic relationship would probably correspond to an illuminated manuscript from Sainte-Marie-de-Lagrasse (Library of Nîmes), an abbey which was closely related to Catalonia. The manuscript belongs to the time of Abbot Robert (1086-1108).

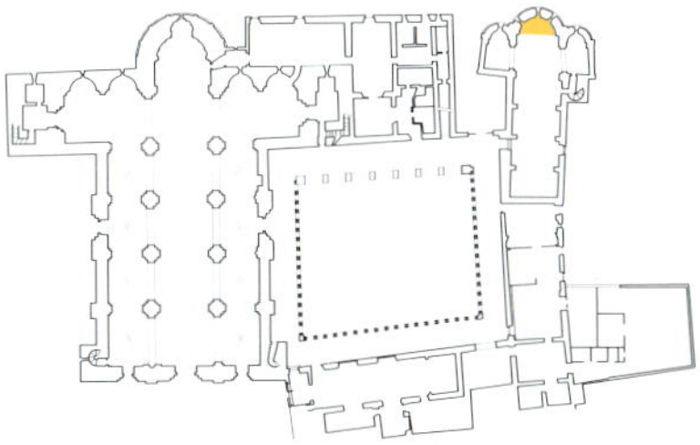

Paintings conserved in the MNAC

2 *Altar from Sant Serni de Tavèrnoles*

12th CENTURY

THE MONASTERY ALTAR from Sant Serni de Tavèrnoles has been reconstructed in the *Apse from Sant Pere in La Seu d'Urgell.* The frontal shows a rhythmic sequence of canonized bishops, wearing mitres and holding croziers. They are presided over by a central figure who is bestowing a blessing. This is probably St. Sernin, the bishop and martyr of Toulouse, after whom the monastery was named, flanked by four canonized bishops. The two figures on the side panels, the bishops Martin and Bricius, clearly reveal that another hand has been at work.

The large dimensions of this piece, sometimes claimed to be a sarcophagus or an altarpiece, also support the theory that it may be the frontal of an altar, since it is identical in width to the *Tavèrnoles Baldachin* (XIII, 124). It is logical to assume that the great size of the church where it was originally installed must also be taken into account.

The unusual iconography has also raised doubts about the function of this piece. It is odd, that instead of depicting the martyrdom of the saint who was dragged by a bull (the capital of the cloister of Moissac, the sarcophagus of Saint-Hilaire, the Rotgers frontal in the Museu Episcopal de Vic), a species of episcopal assembly is portrayed, presided over by Gaul's evangelizing saint. The cult to this saint began in Toulouse (Languedoc), where his martyrdom took place, and where his *passio* was written, and from there spread along the major pilgrimage routes, such as the one to Santiago de Compostela.

3 *Altar frontal from La Seu d'Urgell, also known as the Apostles frontal*

FIRST HALF OF THE 12th CENTURY

THE FRONTAL, WHICH comes from a church in the Urgell diocese, is one of the oldest masterpieces in the panel painting collection. The *Maiestas Domini* is in the centre of the composition, seated on the vault of Heaven with the Earth as a footstool. Christ is within a double mandorla in the Carolingian tradition, very similar to the *Frontal from Ix* (Hix, Cerdagne) (4). The Apostles are on each side, forming two areas that have little to do with the background: the composition of each area is organised by the arrangement of each group of figures. Other characteristics are the intensity of the colour, the quality of the drawing and the sureness of the line. There is a vivacious quality in the eyes of the personages. The rhythmic, geometric arrangement of the folds of the drapery should also be emphasized: some with what has been called a 'flying fold' because of their unique shape.

The great stylistic similarity between both frontals would probably indicate that they came from the same workshop, most likely from in and around Urgell's episcopal seat. Perhaps this would explain not only its relationship with the painting from the *Apse from Sant Pere in La Seu d'Urgell* (1), but also that the stylistic referents are to be found in miniature painting. It is in this sense that illuminated manuscripts from diverse places have been cited, for example the ones in the Gospels of Vic (Arxiu Episcopal de Vic), the Gospels from Cuixà (Saint-Michel de Cuxa, Conflent) (Médiathèque de Perpignan), the *Moralia in Job* by St. Gregory (Arxiu Episcopal de Vic) and in the *Rodes Bible* (Bibliothèque Nationale in Paris). Nevertheless, the illumination which is most akin to it in style is found in a Gospels of unknown origin, most likely from the north of Catalonia or Languedoc, now in the Walters Art Gallery in Baltimore.

An analysis of the pigments has revealed the presence of cinnabar in the red pigment. Cinnabar, obtained from mercury, was imported from southern Spain, then under Islamic rule.

9 *The origins of Catalan coinage*

9.3

9.5

THE INFLUENCE OF the Carolingian monetary system, based on the minting of the silver *diner* (9.1) and the obol, half its value, and widespread throughout western Christianity, determined the origin of Catalan coinage in medieval times. The first Carolingian kings minted coins in the towns of Catalonia themselves, beginning with the first coins issued by Charlemagne (768-814) in Barcelona, Girona, Empúries and Roses, towns that formed part of the 'Marca Hispanica' of the Carolingian Empire. However, at the end of the 10th century and at the beginning of the 11th, the weakening of royal power favoured the independence of Catalan lands, and the counts' appropriation of the minting rights. Their coins, imitating Carolingian coins at first, used a very simple schematic design (9.2); the counts later issued coins in their own name. In fact, the counts even went so far as to delegate the right to mint coins in favour of a number of bishops (9.3).

While the Christian states minted chiefly silver money, the Islamic world used a much more complex monetary system, based on the issue of gold (9.4), silver and copper coins. The signs engraved on these coins were epigraphic, and the content mainly religious. The prestige of the Islamic gold coin meant that at the beginning of the 11th century, some Catalan counts, such as the Count of

Barcelona, exceptionally minted a new gold coin, the *mancús* **(9.5)**, inspired by coins from Al-Andalus, although their inscriptions were usually simplified signs, and sometimes lacked all meaning.

19 *Caliphal capital*

C. 964-965
(IN KEEPING WITH THE INSCRIPTION, THE PERIOD OF CALIPH AL-HAKAM II [961-976])

THIS CAPITAL FROM Cordoba —probably from the Alcazar— pertains to one of the most active periods in Hispano-Islamic art, the period of the Caliphate of Abd al-Rahman III and Al-Hakam II, as do the other Islamic capitals exhibited.

The overall structure indicates a relation to the Late Roman tradition which was present in the southern Iberian Peninsula during the Visigothic rule. For example, we see a design derived from the traditional Corinthian order: two rows of acanthus leaves in the semicircular part, and volutes in the upper corners. The absence of necking is also characteristic; it must have formed part of the shaft of the column. On the whole, the relief has been executed by means of the trepanning technique, although bevelled carving has been used for a few details. The decorative texture is determined by the contrast between light and dark, and between the flat and smooth motifs and the background. The acanthus leaves display volume only on the upper part at the point where they fold over and overhang the bell, in contrast to the classical capital.

The inscription alluding to the Caliph Al-Hakam II and to his minister —

located in the abacus as was the custom— is what permits its classification and explains the dating of the capital. This capital presents a clear analogy to others of the time, and could come from the period when remodelling was undertaken in the Alcazar of Cordoba between the years 964 and 965 —in the year 353 of the Hegira era. This fact confers a great value to the piece because of its uniqueness.

22 *Imposts from the Cathedral of Barcelona*

11th CENTURY

THESE TWO PIECES are associated to the building of the Cathedral of Barcelona in the 11th century, a date deduced from the year the consecration of the Cathedral took place, in 1058. More fragments from the period of construction are conserved in the Museu d'Història de la Ciutat in Barcelona. The motifs (semipalmettes, geometric shapes) and the type of relief —reduced to two planes by the bevelled carving— are characteristic of the sculpture of the 11th century, as has been mentioned in the introduction to this section. The nearest parallels that can be drawn from the imposts of the Cathedral are the reliefs of the Church of Sant Pere de les Puel·les —also in Barcelona— and the ones in Sant Pere in Àger (23). They are simple and rough-hewn, especially if compared to other more relevant examples sculpted during the same century such as the lintel of Sant Genís de Fontanes (Saint-Génis-des-Fontaines, Roussillon) and the capitals from Sant Pere de Rodes.

25 *Capital from Sant Pere de Rodes*

11th OR 12th CENTURY

THIS CAPITAL FROM THE Monastery of Sant Pere de Rodes has three decorated sides and a rough-hewn side at the rear, perhaps because it was meant to abut onto another structure. It has been sculpted using the same technique as the pieces seen before: bevelled carving. In this way, it matches with the decoration on the capitals and the imposts of the pillars in the church of Sant Pere de Rodes on which similar palmettes have been carved. Because of this, it has almost always been dated as an 11th-century artefact, and it has even been suggested that it may have originally been in the church ambulatory. Nevertheless, its proportions and its rough-hewn side —visible on the right— enhances the wide-leaf design on the corners, bringing it nearer to other works carved in the Empordà during the 12th and 13th centuries, such as some pieces from Lledó that were also carved using the bevelling technique.

SECTION II

The paintings from the Church of Sant Joan in Boí

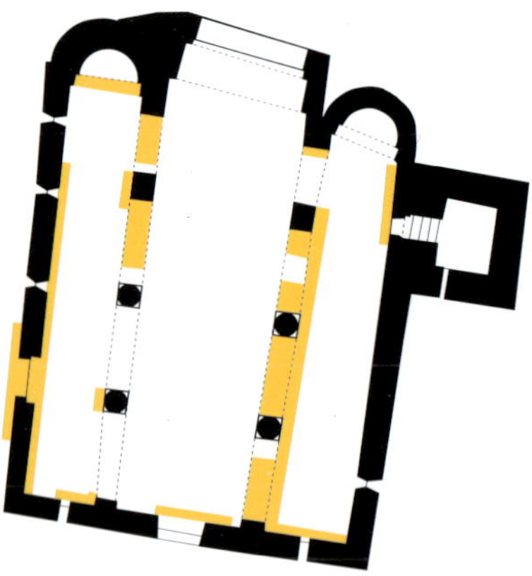

● Paintings conserved in the MNAC

IN THIS SECTION the chronological tour begins and we enter the area dedicated to the extraordinary mural group from the parish church of Sant Joan in Boí **(26)**. The ones from the interior of the church date from *c.* 1100, and those of the façade from the 12th century.

This is the first time that these paintings, some of which were previously unexhibited, have been placed in a space that evokes the church, reproducing its side aisles. The entrance to this section corresponds to the central apse of the church, which has not been preserved. The south side aisle is on the left and the north one is on the right. In both side aisles the paintings are situated in the positions they occupied in the church, except for three panels that are shown out of context. These are separated from the wall to distinguish them clearly from the others.

The side apses have been rebuilt in order to help visitors get their bearings, although their decoration has not been preserved, as is also the case with the central nave. In order to reinforce the notion of the east end of the church, two crucifixes have been placed in the interior of the two apsidioles, although they do not come from this church (28 & 29). There is also an altar stone in the south side aisle **27**.

The paintings from Sant Joan in Boí, dating from *c.* 1100, comprise one of the earliest groups in Catalan Romanesque art. Their dating is in part based on the architecture of the building, and in part on the pictorial evidence from the other churches in the Boí Valley, those of Sant Climent and Santa Maria in Taüll (V) (VII).

On the other hand, the paintings preserved are numerous enough to reveal the importance of the iconographic programmes in Romanesque church interiors. Thus, when referring to the arrangement of the subjects, we can distinguish among the paintings that decorate the perimetral walls, the paintings on the walls which separate the aisles, and the ones on the intradoses of arches.

On the south wall of the church, a quadruped with a serpent-like tail which has a fleur-de-lys in its mouth is exhibited. On the same wall, the panel of *The Stoning of St. Stephen* (26.1) has been placed in order to make it more visible, although this may be to play down the original context. It originally occupied the upper part of the pillar in the same nave, below the roof. As with all the other fragments not placed in their original location, this one is framed. The expressive artistic power of this scene —achieved with such simplicity— is extraordinary. The feeling of movement is obtained by means of the adroit sequential arrangement of the three men who are stoning St. Stephen, thus forming a contrast to the serene attitude of the saint (*'S[ANCTV]S STEFANVS'*).

Likewise, two panels have been sited here with paintings from the west wall. In the panel nearest the stoning, we see a representation of *Heaven and Hell* (26.2). *Heaven* is represented by the souls of the Elect, who are gathered in the bosom of Abraham, as in the Montgauch paintings from the region of Couserans (Gascogne, France); and *Hell*, by monstrous beings who are tormenting a soul. This is an iconographic formula that we shall also see in Santa Maria in Taüll (VII, 102). These two scenes allow us to conclude that the Last Judgement was depicted on the west wall of Boí, as was customary in many churches. In addition to Santa Maria in Taüll, another example of this scene is in the church in Torcello —near Venice— that dates from the end of 11th century and has a very well-preserved iconographic programme. The adjacent panel —also originally from the west wall— shows a figure holding a bird in his hand, perhaps a *Falconer* (26.3).

At the end of the south side aisle, the seven-headed dragon or Beast of the Apocalypse is in its original place. This is a depiction of the devil and the incarnation of evil which will be defeated during the advent of the Kingdom of God (Revelations 20, 7-10).

Nearly all the original decoration of the north wall is preserved, and depicts, from right to left, the Apostle Philip (identified by the remains of an inscription), a minstrel scene, some haloed personages in conversation, and lower down, a frieze depicting zoömorphic figures. The minstrel scene includes two jugglers and a musician, similar to the illustration of a passage in the Book of Daniel in the *Rodes Bible* (Bibliothèque Nationale in Paris), a work from the scriptorium at Ripoll.

Over the series of arches on the wall that separates the aisles, there had been figures of saints, and scenes from their lives (see the figures in the south side aisle, where a complete figure has been preserved). In particular, in the north side aisle above the pillar near the apse, where there is an inscription referring to St. Martin (*'S[ANTV]S MARTINVUS'*) that ought to be accompanied by a scene where the saint appears, equivalent to scene of the *Stoning of St. Stephen* in the south side aisle.

On the intradoses of the arches which separate the side aisles, the remains of a monumental bestiary that is unparalleled in mural painting are preserved. Real and mythical animals are depicted, in addition to a portrayal of a human figure, a lame man. On the other side of the same arch, we see a four-legged animal biting its own tail. On the last intrados on this south side, there is a large bird with two heads. On three consecutive intradoses in the north side aisle, from east to west, important remains of the bestiary are preserved. In the first one there is a lion (identified by the inscription *'LEO'*), an elephant and a fierce-looking quadruped with an inscription (*'CARCOLITI'*) that is difficult to identify with any animal. On the following intrados there is a hybrid of a bird and a fish (*'MAGR* [...]'). And finally on the third intrados another quadruped appears, a tail curled round its body, and beneath, a fragmentary image of a dragon (*'VIPRA'*).

Both the bestiary and the lame man may be of a moralizing nature.

Nearby, in the tympanum over the door of the north wall, there is a cock whose crowing announcing the dawn is a symbol of Christ and the Resurrection, according to the verses of the first hymn of the *Cathemerinon* by Prudentius, a Christian poet from the 4th century.

Around the exterior portal of the church, and chronologically later than it, there is a not very well-preserved Theophany with, in its lower part, graffiti with scenes of a military character; these are also medieval but done later than the paintings.

A study of the pigments and the techniques utilized indicates, not only that the pictorial procedure was not very rigorous, but also that the pigments are poorer in quality than those used in the paintings at Pedret and Taüll. Only local pigments mixed with clay were used.

As far as style is concerned, there have been no similarities established between the Sant Joan in Boí paintings and other Catalan examples. However, similarities have been found with some aspects of the paintings from Saint-Martin de Vicq (Nohant-Vicq, Indre, in the centre of France) done in the second half of the 12th century. This was less a result of interdependence than the influence of common European models, perhaps Carolingian, on local traditions. The same thing is noticeable when the iconography of the Boí minstrel figures are compared to the ones in the *Rodes Bible.* This can be explained by the assumption of common sources, but the coincidences are too few to establish a direct influence. Therefore, the Boí paintings could be viewed as an example of an existing tradition in Catalonia, separate from the Italian influence represented by the Pedret paintings (III), which we will see in the following section.

27 *Altar stone from Castellet*

10th CENTURY

THE ALTAR IS THE CENTRAL element in the furnishing of any church since it is the place where the Eucharist is celebrated. It was usually made up of one or more supports (probably piece **5** in section **I** was an altar support), on which a crafted rectangular slab rested. This was often a reused block of marble. The altar stone from Sant Esteve in Castellet, also known as Les Masuques altar stone, is a relatively plain example: the only decoration is the molding framing it. The block is surprisingly thick. Attention should be paid to the engraved inscriptions on the surface: some of them are from the day it was consecrated. Among these, the one which states 'DONADEVS ABBA', Abbot of Sant Cugat del Vallès from 904 to 917, is of note, while his signature also appears on the *Altar stone from Sant Feliuet de Vilamilans* (Vallès Occidental). This inscription implies that the restoration of worship at the Church of Sant Esteve in Castellet can be attributed to him.

SECTION III

The Pedret Circle paintings

JUST AS ROMANESQUE architecture from Lombardy spread throughout Catalonia and a large part of Europe in the 11th century, giving rise to what J. Puig i Cadafalch called 'Early Romanesque Art', so painting from the north of Italy reached Catalonia at the end of the same century. The clearest example of this type of painting is found in the mural group from Sant Quirze in Pedret, and in a series of frescoes closely linked to it stylistically, some of which are conserved in the Museum: Sant Pere in Àger **31**, Santa Maria d'Àneu **37** and Sant Pere in El Burgal **38**.

Of the Pedret paintings, the Museu Diocesà i Comarcal de Solsona conserves the central apse decoration, and the MNAC that which comes from the two side apses. The latter are referred to in the earliest studies of Catalan Romanesque painting, undertaken by F. Muns in 1887 and J. Puiggarí in 1889.

The paintings on the central apse depict the apocalyptic vision of the Throne with the Book of the Seven Seals (Revelations 5-8), the twenty-four enthroned Elders and the four Horsemen of the Apocalypse, corresponding to the opening of the first four Seals, and the souls of the Blessed at the Altar of God during the opening of the Fifth Seal. The apse vaulting shows Christ in Majesty and the Tetramorph. In the chancel, Cain and Abel make their offering to God, and the martyrdom of the patron saints Quiricus and Julitta are depicted. In addition, the sacrifice of Isaac can be seen, and a frieze which includes busts of saints such as Paul, Celsus and Pierius, among others.

On the south, or Epistle side apse **30** —exhibited in the Museum— is the parable of the wise and the foolish Virgins (Matthew 25) in which the wise Virgins are seated at the table of Christ the bridegroom, at the heavenly banquet. According to St. Augustine the parable symbolizes the universal Church, where the bridegroom and bride are symbols of Christ and the Church.

In the Middle Ages such subject matter was linked to the liturgical drama of the *Sponsus,* read at the time of the Advent. This alludes to the Last Judgement, showing the elect souls and those damned to Hell. Moreover, it has a marked ecclesiological character —that is, it refers to the doctrine of the Church as an institution— emphasised by the crowned and haloed figure seated on top of a building representing the Church. On the dome, the Virgin and the Child are enthroned. The portrayal of a seated man writing, in the intrados of the arch, is thought to be St. Matthew the Evangelist.

On the north, or Gospel side apse, the apostolic college is depicted; it has a bearing on the ecclesiological character of the iconographic programme, created at the time of the 11th-century Gregorian reform that vindicated the predominance of the Holy See over temporal power.

Of the two iconographic cycles of the Apocalypse found in the European art of the time, the Pedret group is the one that does not belong to the Hispanic tradition which engendered the *Beatus* miniature, but rather to the European trend which arose from Italian examples from Late Antiquity and the early Middle Ages.

Apse from Santa Maria d'Àneu

The cycle has its antecedents in Italy: in the baptistry of the Cathedral of Novara (*c.* 1000), in San Pietro al Monte in Civate (from about the end of the 11th century to the beginning of the 12th), and in Castel Sant'Elia (at the same time as the latter), and some time afterward in the Cathedral of Anagni. In Catalonia, this can also be seen in the *Rodes Bible* and in the Fenollar murals (Saint-Martin-de-Fenouillar, Vallespir) and Polinyà.

Detail of Countess Llúcia on the apse from Sant Pere in El Burgal

The subjects represented on the two large apses, linked in style to the Italian school represented by the Pedret Circle, Santa Maria d'Àneu and Sant Pere in El Burgal, also show this influence from the north of Italy.

On El Burgal apse vaulting, the *Maiestas Domini* can be seen, and on that of Àneu, the Virgin Mary and Child are placed within the mandorla as a manifestation of the Incarnation of Christ and the explanation of both the divine and human nature of Christ, the hypostatic union. The Virgin, as *Sedes Sapientiae*, represents the human nature and acquires a fundamental role in the scene of the Epiphany.

In both the El Burgal and the Àneu frecoes, the iconographic programme alludes to the Old Testament through the presence of the prophets in reverential attitudes, as occurs in San Vicenzo in Galliano, dated a short time after the year 1000. On the apse from El Burgal, the *Maiestas Domini* was flanked by two prophets on the vaulting. Elijah and Isaiah appear on the apse of Santa Maria d'Àneu. In keeping with Isaiah's vision, there are six-winged seraphims who purify the mouths of the prophets with fire so that their words may be turned into the Word of God. In addition, the wheels of fire from Jehovah's chariot are depicted, conforming to Ezekiel's vision.

The archangels Gabriel and Michael, dressed in the Byzantine Empire style, can be seen in both apses. They carry a banner and scrolls with the inscriptions '*PETICIVS*' and '*POSTVLACIVS*', which designate them as intercessory archangels entrusted with seeking God's pardon for the sins of men. These characteristics are frequent in north Italian painting, for instance in San Vicenzo in Galliano, and also in Catalonia: El Burgal, Àneu Esterri de Cardós **(IV, 44)**, Estaon **(XI, 117)** and Tredós (The Cloisters in New York).

Other features that link these groups to each other and to the north of Italy, are the decorative borders and the simulated drapery, which in Pedret, El Burgal and Àneu have waves and circular medallions of a marked classical character. A geometrical border in relief like the one in San Carlo in Prugiasco (Negrentino, Switzerland, 11th century) and in San Orso (Aosta, beginning of the 12th century) can be found in Pedret, El Burgal and Sant Vicenç in Rus (Museu Diocesà i Comarcal in Solsona); the latter are somewhat later than those of the Pedret Circle. In El Burgal, this border has an alternating ornamental motif identified as the crown of Monza, the symbol of royal power in Lombardy. Furthermore, the presence of various saints venerated in the Milan Church would corroborate a relationship with the region of Lombardy. Thus for example, the Milanese saint Pierius appears in Pedret; Gervasius and Protasius are in Tredós and in Sorpe **(IX, 115)**, where Ambrosius, the patron saint of the Milan Church, also appears.

Stylistically, the Pedret paintings are of an extraordinary quality, and historiography has linked them to the Italian groups from Galliano as well as from San Pietro al Monte in Civate, and San Carlo in Prugiasco.

This influence of northern Italy will also be found in Taüll, but without the classical touch of Pedret. The paintings from the *Apse of Sant Climent in Taüll* **(V, 68)** are more geometrical, more symmetrically organised, following the accepted canons.

The Museum technical services have analysed the pigments utilised in Pedret (the side apses paintings), El Burgal and Àneu. A better technical command has been observed in Pedret, both in the regularity of the pictorial layer and in the grinding and uniform distribution of the pigments. The technical differences among the aforementioned groups would indicate the presence of several hands at work. Furthermore, the relationship of the three groups is clear when the paintings are seen under an electronic microscope, both in the quality of the pigments and in their preparation, suggesting that different yet stylistically closely related painters worked on them. Azurite was used for blue in the two frescoes from Àneu and El Burgal. This is a very costly mineral not available in the area: it must have been imported, perhaps by the painters themselves. Azurite is the same mineral used in the north of Italy, for example in San Pietro al Monte in Civate. Aerinite, a material found in the Pyrenees, was used for blue in Taüll. Therefore, we have a group of painters linked to a prevailing international tendency which arrived from the north of Italy, in particular from the region of Lombardy and from the vicinity of Milan. These painters introduced an art in Catalonia that broke with the continuity of earlier local traditions in some ways. Later on, the art of these painters would be imitated by those working in Orcau **(40)** and in Argolell **(41)**.

The chronological coordinates of the so-called Pedret Circle are derived from secondary information. The arrival of this style in Catalonia can, broadly speaking, be situated in the last third of the 11th century, and the influence of this style continued into the next century. One of the chronological points of reference is the donor of Sant Pere in El Burgal, who was identified by Joan Ainaud as the Countess Llúcia de Pallars, wife of Artau I, who took charge of the government of the county when she was widowed in 1081. Her portrayal on this apse —the first female portrait in the Museum— corresponds in all likelihood to the period of her widowhood (1081-1090). Another example of this tradition of portraying the donor, which has precedents in Byzantine art and in the early Middle Ages, is the *Donoress of Sant Pere in Esterri d'Àneu* **(39)**.

An additional piece of information for the dating of this stylistic ensemble is the document of covenant and endowment from the Church of Santa Maria d'Àneu **37**, signed on 30 March 1085 by Count Artau II and the bishop Bernat of Urgell.

Moreover, the construction of the collegiate church in Àger, from which we include two magnificent Apostles dressed in classical fashion, may have been finished in 1079 because that is the date that the testament of the presbyter, Adalbert, was read from the altar. The stylistic relationship that historiography has established among these paintings and those of the Cathedral of Saint-Lizier, Couserans (Gascogne, France), consecrated in 1117, furnishes us with another chronological reference.

All this information helps to determine the dates of the earliest work from the Pedret Circle as being near the end of the 11th century.

30 *Side apses from Pedret*

END OF THE 11th CENTURY

THE ICONOGRAPHIC PROGRAMME of the Church of Sant Quirze in Pedret is very rich and complex, as has been explained in the introduction to this section. The programme is of an apocalyptic type in the paintings on the central apse (Museu Diocesà i Comarcal de Solsona); and of an ecclesiological character in the side apses exhibited here. The left apse shows the assembled Apostles around Peter, representing the Church as an institution and also the supremacy of Rome. On the right —much better-preserved— is one of the jewels of the collection. It depicts the famous parable of the wise and the foolish Virgins; on

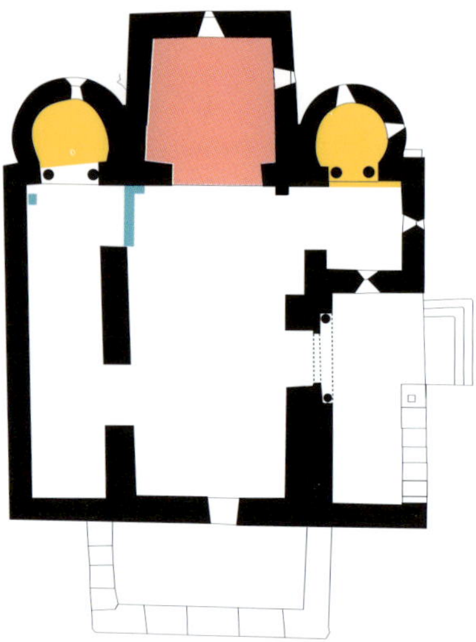

Paintings conserved in the MNAC
Paintings conserved *in situ*
Paintings conserved in the Museu Diocesà i Comarcal de Solsona

the intrados of the arch is St. Matthew the Evangelist, who wrote the parable down (Matthew 25, 1-13), seated at his writing table. The meaning of the parable is eschatological. It refers to the end of time when only the Christians who are prepared for the Coming of the Lord will be allowed to enter His house. On the apse vaulting, there is a bust of Mary, the most prudent of the virgins and the seat for the Christ Child. The ecclesiological nature of the programme, already evident on the other apse, is reinforced by the image of the Church shaped as a woman seated on a temple.

The study of the pigments has demonstrated the use of aerinite —a mineral compound found in the Pyrenees to obtain blue — in place of azurite, an imported mineral normally used in Lombardy and also in El Burgal and Àneu, which belong to the same stylistic circle. As for the painting technique, they resemble each other when closely observed under an electronic microscope, although the Pedret paintings have been revealed to be superior to those from Àneu and El Burgal.

31 *Apostles from Àger: Thaddaeus and James*

C. 1100

THE CHURCH OF SANT Pere in Àger was the seat of a community of Augustinian canons which possessed vast territorial domains and enjoyed exemption from ordinary diocesan jurisdiction. It was founded and endowed in 1048 by Arnau Mir of Tost, the mythical conqueror of the Àger Valley.

From this canonical, later collegiate Church of Sant Pere in Àger, the monumental figures of the Apostles Thaddaeus (*'S[AN]C[TV]S TADEVS'*) and James (*'S[AN]C[TV]S IACOBVS'*) are conserved. They are dressed in classical attire, in *manicata* and *pallia* tunics that bear an amazing likeness to the apse figures of the former Cathedral of Saint-Lizier, in Couserans (Gascogne, France).

34 *Crozier*

C. 1230-40

CROZIERS ARE a sign of the authority and dignity of bishops and abbots. They can be made from several types of material, such as ivory, wood, metal and so forth. In many cases they were wrought of copper and enamel, like those from Limoges **(XV)**. Here, the staff is of unknown origin. As usually occurs, only the upper part has been preserved; it is comprised of the volute, the knob, and the shaft that holds the staff in place. Of the diverse decorative features, the one that should be pointed out is the volute, designed with reptilian shapes and finished off with the head of a serpent, a very frequent kind of decoration which this crozier shares with other pieces exhibited in the same showcase. Traditionally the serpent motif has been related to the episode of the brazen serpent (Numbers 21, 6-9), and also to the miraculous transformation of Aaron's staff into a serpent before the very eyes of the Pharaoh (Exodus 7, 9-12). In these episodes, the serpent is a symbol of sainthood. The centre of the volute usually displayed openwork decoration —missing, in this case— which might be floral, zoömorphic, or a narrative scene. The adjacent examples show two of the most frequent subjects: St. Michael slaying the dragon **(33)**, (as in the *Mondoñedo crozier* **(XV, 134)** and the Annunciation **(35)**. As far as the rest of the decoration is concerned, the enamelling can be appreciated on both the shaft and the volute itself, where the lapis lazuli blue surfaces predominate.

37 *Apse from Santa Maria d'Àneu*

END OF THE 11th CENTURY

THESE PAINTINGS ARE FROM Santa Maria d'Àneu, the seat of an Augustinian canonical community. The iconographic programme of the apse is very rich and complex. On its semicircular part, there are some superb monumental seraphim —the wings replete with eyes— who purify the words of the prophets Elijah and Isaiah (identified from the remains of different inscriptions) with burning coals held in tongs, according to Isaiah's vision (6, 1-3, 6-7). The eyes signify that God is all-knowing and all-seeing, whilst the triple *Sanctus* being intoned is a song of praise to the Lord. Between the two prophets are the wheels of fire from Jehovah's chariot as described by Ezekiel (10, 1-22). The paintings on the vaulting, partially lost, represent the fulfilment of the biblical prophecies, with Mary holding the Messiah on her lap as she presents him to the Magi, who have come to pay homage to the Christ Child. At the sides, the archangels Michael and Gabriel appear: Michael holds the banner of Christ, while the figure of Gabriel is too deteriorated to discern very much. On the right, in the semicircular area, the archangel Raphael can be seen. On the left, two clerics are depicted as donors. The building of the church and the creation of the paintings may be related to a written agreement between the Bishop of Urgell and the Count of Pallars signed in 1085.

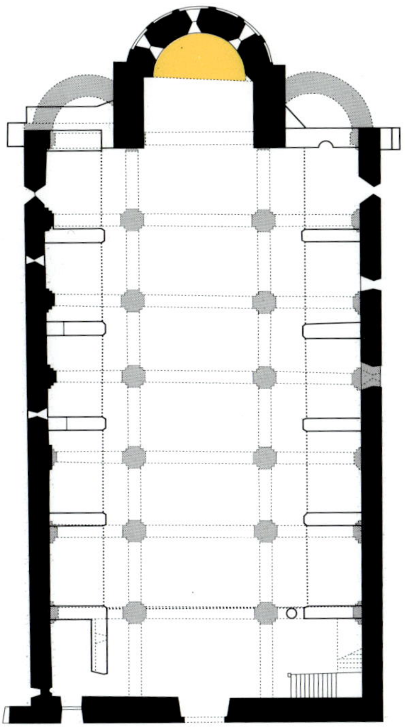

Paintings conserved in the MNAC

38 *Apse from El Burgal*

END OF THE 11th CENTURY

THE APSE IS FROM the church of the former Benedictine monastery of Sant Pere in El Burgal. The hieratic rigidity of the figures on the semicircular area and on the triumphal arch is impressive. The saints and apostles who represent the Church have a Byzantine look, in vivid contrast to the gracefulness of the two Old Testament prophets bowing to the *Maiestas Domini.* The programme developed on this apse has an evident eucharistic and ecclesiological meaning, perfectly illustrated in the four central figures: Peter, Mary, John the Baptist and Paul. Peter, of whom Christ said 'Thou that art Peter, and upon this rock I will build my church' (Matthew 16, 18) is counterposed to Paul, the apostle of the Gentiles. Mary is transformed into an image representing the Church by holding the chalice that symbolizes the Eucharist. On the other side of the window, John the Baptist, the Precursor, carries the Lamb in his arms, symbol of the dead and resurrected Jesus Christ. At the bottom, is the portrayal of the Countess Llúcia of Pallars, the sister of Countess Almodis of Barcelona, and widow of Artau I, Count of Pallars between 1081 and 1090, thus enabling us to date the paintings.

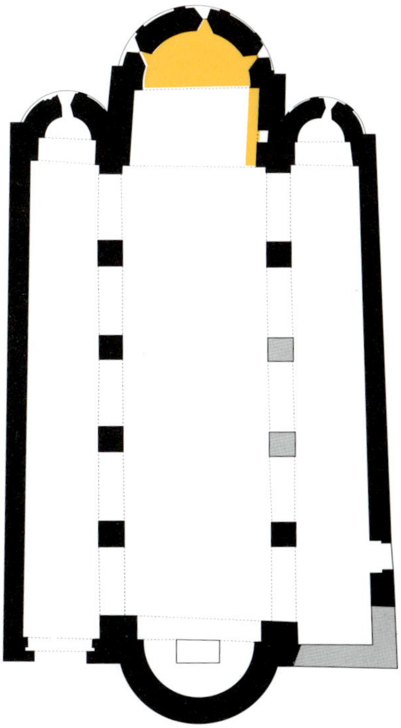

Paintings conserved in the MNAC

SECTION IV

Christ and Mary in iconography

IN THIS SECTION the chronological and stylistic discourse has been interrupted to take up aspects related to iconography, or the study of images and their meanings. In particular, the pieces in this section permit us to grasp some of the more important subjects relating to Jesus Christ as the central figure of Christianity, as well as to the dogmas of Incarnation and Redemption. The figure of Mary in relation to Christ is emphasized, and in large part she becomes a symbol of the Church. It must be added that the programmes of images of the time oriented towards the kinds of artefacts displayed here, and having preferential status within the church building itself, were determined by their synthetic and solemn nature. As a consequence, the use of biblical texts and sources extends beyond any narrative ambition.

Thus, the actual order of the works will enable us to analyse, in the first group, those compositions devoted to the Ascension of Christ, the depictions of Christ in Majesty, and the Death and Resurrection of Christ. Those issues related to the Virgin Mary and the Infant Jesus, plus other aspects concerning the figure of Mary as a whole will be dealt with in the second group.

The first two groups of wall paintings, the *Apse from Mur* (42) and the *Apse from Marmellar* (43), present the Ascension of Jesus Christ, that is to say, His triumph and His return to the right hand of God the Father, Christ's Elevation to Glory. This subject seldom appears on Catalan apses of the Romanesque age, excepting the possible allusion which appears on the *Apse from Sant Pere in La Seu d'Urgell* (I, 1). In Catalonia, this subject has been found on panel paintings: for instance, on the *Frontal from Martinet de Cerdanya* (Worcester Art Museum, Massachusetts). Among other early European examples, a few sculpted French tympanums can be cited, such as the no longer extant Abbey of Cluny.

In Mur the depiction of the Ascension is on the vault of the south side apse of the church. The figure of Christ is inscribed within the mandorla, surrounded by billowing clouds. The fact that the figure appears in profile allows us to relate it to Carolingian works. Furthermore, the disk-shaped object in His hand —which may have a eucharistic meaning— is also a reminder of the Carolingian world. Mary and the disciples, witnesses to the Ascension, appear below, as is customary in the semicircular area. Bearing in mind the biblical text —Acts of the Apostles 1, 9-11—, this episode can be interpreted as an announcement of the Second Parousia —the Second Coming of Jesus Christ— which is precisely on the central apse of Mur (Museum of Fine Arts, Boston).

These paintings are said to be related in style to French tendencies, although their nearest counterpart are the paintings in the chapel of Saint-Marie in Arles (Arles-sur-Tech, Vallespir) dated about the year 1157. On the other hand, the *Apse from Marmellar* is characterized by a technical crudeness so extreme that it impedes any study of it in relation to the major tendencies of the period.

The composition of the *Apse from Marmellar* —difficult to interpret— depicts an Ascension of a Theophanic character. Christ is standing within the mandorla, directly facing the spectator, above a procession of figures. Moreover, the composition and the figures are treated rather clumsily, which makes the interpretation of the other scenes even more difficult.

Following this there is a series of pieces, in particular the apses and the altar frontals, where portrayals of the *Maiestas Domini*, surrounded by the Tetramorph and by several hierarchies of angels, can be seen. This is a Theophanic vision relating to the Second Coming of Christ, based mainly on the vision of St. John, but there are other biblical references as well. Some of the iconographic features shown here have already been observed in works exhibited in earlier sections of the exhibition. The apses from Esterri de Cardós **44** and Ginestarre (46) follow the same scheme. In the first, the presence of the interceding archangels should be underlined. They present Christ in His role as judge, as we have seen in Santa Maria d'Àneu (III, 37), and as we shall see later in Estaon (XI, 117). However, notable milestones like the *Apse from Sant Climent in Taüll* (V, 68) should not be forgotten. The importance which is usually conceded to Mary and to St. Paul is emphasized on the lower part of the apses of Esterri de Cardós and Ginestarre, on the semicircular wall.

The depiction of Christ in Majesty and the Tetramorph in a traditional hierarchical arrangement is also seen in some of the church furnishings, such as the altar frontals and the baldachin panels. The baldachin panel from Tost **47** is an example related in style to other works done later. This exhibit gives the visitor the chance to compare three pieces executed with distinct techniques: firstly, the stucco relief on the *Frontal from Esterri de Cardós* **45**; secondly, the wood carving on the *Frontal from Benavent* (48); and finally, panel painting, which is represented in this section by the so-called *Frontal from Esquius* **49**, a work we shall analyse further because the inscriptions are of interest. On the *Frontal from Benavent* —a very late work having a coat of polychromy added at an even later date— the shapes on the frame are reminders of the applications of precious stones that used to be included on the frontals made of precious metals —usually gold; this has been documented in several cathedrals and monasteries of the period. This question is commented on later in the passages dedicated to the pieces of metalwork and enamelling (XV). The *Christ in Majesty from Basarán* (54), which must have formed part of a no longer extant altar frontal, could have had the same iconographic design as the *Maiestas Domini*. Next to this work, a wooden fragment of an Italian cross **55** shows Christ surrounded by angels.

Other pieces deal with the death of Christ, and to a lesser extent, the Resurrection. The image of Christ on the Cross symbolizes the Redemption of humanity, a central idea of Christianity. Furthermore, the Crucifixion suggests the Fall of man, whilst Christ is the new Adam (Adam is sometimes portrayed at the foot of the cross). The image of Christ on the Cross has given rise to several typological variants which are analysed later (VIII). As an example of this theme, we see the *Majesty from Éller* (52) and the *Christ from Cabdella* (50). At the conclusion of this selection of crucifixes, we see a gilded bronze figure of *Christ* (56), but without the Cross. In addition, the frequent presence of Mary and John at Calvary should be noted: they are to the right and left of Christ respectively, as in the *Calvary from Tragó de Noguera* **53**. These figures are seen on other objects, such as crosses **57** and covers of books (58), notably Gospels and sacramentaries.

Proceeding through this section we see the reverse side of the polychromed *Cross from Bagergue* (51). The Lamb of God depicts the idea of Christ's redemptive sacrifice. The cross and the banner which allude to the Resurrection also refer to the idea of triumph. The inscriptions reinforce the idea of the sacrifice and triumph of Jesus Christ over death. The Resurrection is represented more plainly on a châsse which depicts the three Marys at the Tomb of Christ (59).

The subject matter and contents relating to the figure of Christ do not end with the pieces exhibited in this part of the section. However, some fundamental ideas have been introduced. The part the figures of Christ and Mary play, will be taken up again in the second part of this explanation.

44 *Apse from Esterri de Cardós*

SECOND HALF OF THE 12th CENTURY

THE APSE PAINTING from the parish church of Sant Pau in Esterri de Cardós, located in the Cardós Valley, has been preserved. On the vaulting there is a very complete Theophany inspired by the Book of Revelation and other biblical sources, as has been explained in the introduction to this section. Christ in Majesty, between Alpha and Omega, represents the beginning and the end of all things. He makes a gesture of blessing with His right hand and holds the book of life in His left. The Tetramorph is placed round the mandorla: the angel for Matthew and the eagle for John, and below, the ox for Luke and the lion for Mark, in a centrifugal arrangement, just as was done in early Byzantine art: in the mosaic on the apse of the Church of Hagios David, in Salonika, and in Merovingian examples such as the sarcophagus of Bishop Angilbert, in Jouarre. On both sides stand an identical thurifer cherubim and seraphim whose wings are covered in eyes. These eyes signify that God sees all and knows all. At each end, the interceding archangels are portrayed: Gabriel on the right, next to a barely legible inscription (*'POSTVLACIVS'*), and Michael on the left, next to the less well-preserved the vestiges of the inscription he was holding. On the lower part of the vision, there are a series of objects of eucharistic and eulogistic meaning: chalices, censers, horns. Below, on the semicircular wall, the Apostles were to be seen flanking the central figures of Mary and Paul, the Apostle of the Gentiles. Paul, who in the paintings from Orcau and Argolell **(III, 40-41)** holds a book with a quotation from the Acts of the Apostles (*'VAX ELICIONIS EST MIHI'*) (Acts of the Apostles 9, 15), in this depiction he holds a kind of goblet that alludes to his own nature as a chosen vessel of the Lord. The paintings from Esterri de Cardós have a certain similarity to the ones from the Ginestarre apse **(46)** —especially the facial features— which in spite of their variations are a popular derivation of the style from the Pedret Circle.

45 *Altar frontal from Esterri de Cardós*

1225 (AS STATED IN THE INSCRIPTION ON THE BEVELLING OF THE RIGHT SIDE OF THE FRAME)

THIS ALTAR FRONTAL is located inside the apse from Sant Pau in Esterri de Cardós. A Christ in Majesty is in the centre surrounded by the Tetramorph, the Apostles on each side. The stucco figures in relief were laminated in yellow-varnished silver, simulating gold, as if the frontal were an example of the goldsmith's art. The metal has rusted and disintegrated with time, but the original relife has been preserved intact, along with the red and green background colours. During the recent restoration in 1995, paint was discovered beneath the frame. This suggests that the panels could have been used in an older altar. The present altar, executed later than the apsidal paintings **(44)**, is dated 1225 from the time of Christ's Incarnation according to an inscription (*«AB INCARNACIONE CHRISTI MCCXXV»*) on the inner bevelling of the right side of the frame. The inscriptions on the upper bevelling refer to the figures of the Apostles Matthew, Barnabas and Paul on the left, and to Peter, Andrew and Thomas who appear on the right, in addition to the symbols of the Evangelists Matthew and John which appear on the upper part. The inscriptions on the lower part no longer exist. A very similar example to the frontal from Esterri de Cardós is the one from Ginestarre conserved in The Cloisters, New York.

47 *Baldachin from Tost*

C. 1200

A BALDACHIN IS the ornamental canopy situated over the altar to add relevance to the most important place in the church, the place where the Eucharist is celebrated. There are two types: panels tilted over the altar, as is shown here, which is from the parish church of Sant Martí in Tost, and the *Tavèrnoles*

Baldachin (XIII, 124); or it can be a shrine on columns, like the so-called *Baldachin from Toses* (V, 81).

Christ in Majesty is depicted on the *Baldachin from Tost*. He holds a book which has the inscription '*EGO S[VM] LUX MUNDI*' (John 8, 12), 'I am the light of the world', which refers to salvation. The symbols of the Tetramorph that circle him are the bearers of the divine word. The four figures are highly adapted to the space provided by the spandrels (or the bevelled triangles) that complement the mandorla, and which are a typical feature of Romanesque art. Recent cleaning of the piece has recovered the luminosity of the original flat colours, defined by thick black outlines, as in the stained-glass window technique.

The crossbeam and the cresting of the baldachin depicting the Last Supper is conserved in the Museu Episcopal de Vic. On the rear side of this beam, the signs of the zodiac and bestiary are placed within medallion shapes which are reminiscent of those on the so-called *Baldachin from Toses* (V, 81).

The *Baldachin from Tost* is stylistically related to other works from the artistic renewal of 1200.

49 *The so-called altar frontal from Esquius*

SECOND HALF OF 12th CENTURY

IN THE BIBLIOGRAPHY THIS PIECE is also known as the Espona frontal because it comes from the Espona Collection (Esquius has not been identified as a place). It presents the most characteristic iconography of this type of work done in the 12th century, along with work sometimes executed in the 13th, such as the *Frontal from Benavent* **(48)**. *The so-called altar frontal from Esquius* shows Christ in Majesty within the mandorla, circled by the symbols of the Four Evangelists. On the sides, in two subdivided compartments, one above the other, the Apostles stand out on a background painted with bands of colour; this is often found in wall painting but not very often in panel painting. The inscription on the mandorla contains an invocation to God, who is the beginning and the end, full of mercy, pity and forgiveness: His charity loosens the chains of the wretched: *'HIC DEVS ALFA EI O[MEGA] CLEMENS MISERATOR ADESTO / AC PIETATE TVA MISERORVM VINCLA RELAXA AMEN'.*

This frontal is the one most closely related to the *Baldachin from Ribes* in style (Museu Episcopal de Vic), one of the best works in Catalan Romanesque painting, where the same range of colours and some palaeographic characters are repeated. Moreover, other similarities, albeit vaguer, have been found with the *Apse from Sant Pere in La Seu d'Urgell,* and with the frontals from La Seu d'Urgell and Ix (Hix, Cerdagne) **(I, 1, 3 & 4)**. The figures in the lower corners exhibit an earlier pictorial intervention (see especially the robes of the Apostles at either extremity), already extant when the frontal was exhibited in the Universal Exposition of Barcelona in 1888.

53 *Calvary from Tragó de Noguera*

SECOND HALF OF THE 13th CENTURY

DESPITE ITS PLAIN and uncomplicated carving, the *Calvary from Tragó de Noguera* is an important piece, as much for the typology that it represents as for its acceptable state of preservation. Furthermore, the last restoration that was done allowed to emphasize some details and its polychromy, which was darkened by the passage of time.

The Calvaries are known by the presence of the figures of Mary and John the Evangelist beside the crucified Christ (John 19, 25-27). On this piece, the figures of Mary and St. John are added to each side of the horizontal bar of the cross. However, on some occasions these figures are painted, as in the *Salardú Christ* in the Aran Valley and that from Sant Martí in Envalls, Cerdanya (Institut Amatller d'Art Hispànic, Barcelona). The figure of Adam leaving his tomb has also been applied separately to the work. Adam is just under Christ's feet because, according to tradition, he was buried in Golgotha, in the very same place where Jesus was crucified. This depiction of Adam signified that he would be redeemed by the death of Christ, in spite of his sin.

The reverse side of the cross, which cannot be seen, is decorated with the figure of the *Agnus Dei*, as occurs on the *Cross from Bagergue* **(51)**.

55 *Fragment of an Italian cross*

SECOND HALF OF THE 13th CENTURY

THE FINE DETAIL, the pictorial quality, the colours and the drawing in this small fragment depicting Christ in Majesty, reveal that it was Italian-made. It probably comes from the region of Las Marcas, in central Italy. Several crosses from the 13th century come from this area. They all have a crosspiece which displays a kind of transverse crest with this depiction of Christ in Majesty seated on a cushioned throne within a mandorla and accompanied by angels and seraphim. This image, situated over the crucified Christ, represents the triumphal return of Jesus Christ to judge the living and the dead. The fragment exhibited must have corresponded to such a formula, in which the mandorla is held up by angels.

57 *Christ on the Cross*

C. 1190

THIS SOLID CROSS is made of enamelled copper and is one of the most interesting and studied pieces in the collection. Where it comes from is unknown, a circumstance that is shared by many pieces of metalwork in the Museum. The reason for this is that many of them were acquired by collectors in the antiques market. The cross is comprised of the customary elements: a suffering seminaked crucified Christ; the busts of Mary and John; the hand of God; and Adam rising from his tomb, as we have observed in the *Calvary from Tragó de Noguera* (53). The reverse side, with the figure of the *Agnus Dei* in the centre, has a vermiculated background of wavy lines, which might be an allusion to the Tree of Life.

This cross belongs to a group of objects from Limoges attributed to the so-called Master of Chiselled Asters, who is characterized by his handling of such aster-tipe floral motifs using the technique of chiselling.

THE TWO SHOWCASES on the left introduce the second group of works, which begins with wood carvings portraying Mary and the Infant Jesus. Thus, in the 12th-century images of the Virgin and Child, the former is enthroned as *Sedes Sapientiae* (namely the Seat of Wisdom), and as *Sedes Christi (*the Throne of Christ). They are compositions characterized by hieratism, a rigidity of postures and gestures, and a symmetrical tendency. At the same time, Mary represents the Church. Works like the *Virgin from Ger* **61** and the *Virgin from Matadars* **(64)**, reproduce this scheme. The latter has been compared to the *Virgin of Montserrat* because of its composition on a more monumental scale, and by the structure of the throne.

As time went by, some features began to suggest the role of Mary as mother, such as in the image of the Virgin where the breasts and abdomen are slightly accentuated **(62)**. At the same time, some examples —the figure of the Child seen side-on— break up the rigidity of the composition. Nevertheless, the forerunners of this design might come from earlier periods (the *Virgin from Imad*, from Paderborn). This is the case of another image of unknown origin **(63)**, executed in a rudimentary and awkward way, which has been linked to the stone sculpture of the *Virgin of the Solsona Cloister*, attributed to the sculptor of the school of Toulouse, Gilabertus. These similarities allow a connection to be made among some wood carvings and the stone sculptures.

Furthermore, it should not be forgotten that some of these images of the Virgin and the Infant Jesus were utilised in liturgical dramas, as in the *Officium Stellae*, a work in which the Adoration of the Magi was performed on the day of Epiphany.

The adoration of the Virgin gradually increased, influenced by the social and historical changes that were taking place in Europe, which were already linked to the new Gothic spirit. Little by little, the single figure of Mary gained in importance in Western Europe, especially during the 13th century.

Thus, in some altar frontals, especially those from a later period, the growing relevance of the compositions of the Virgin and the Child is discerned, as in the subject of the *Maiestas Mariae,* situated in the central compartment. Surrounded by angels and depicted within the mandorla, it acquires a sense of Theophany. This is also the case of the *Frontal from Alós d'Isil* **(65)**, where the main subject is the glorification of Mary, and it occurs as well in the sculpted tympanum in Cornellà de Conflent (Corneilla de Conflent). Nevertheless, it should be pointed out that this composition derives from earlier examples. The image is meant mainly to emphasize the principle of the Incarnation: Christ as a man.

The presence of the Tetramorph can be interpreted as a confirmation of the Incarnation, the idea of Mary as Mother of God, since the Four Evangelists are witnesses. Thus, the episodes from Christ's infancy depicted on the lateral areas of the frontals also have to do with the divine Incarnation. The Tetramorph can also be understood as a symbol of permanence and eternity of the Dominion of the Church. The *Frontal from Cardet* **66** continues this same idea, as does the *Frontal from El Coll* (Museu Episcopal de Vic).

On the *Frontal from Cardet*, a crowned Mary appears as Queen of Heaven. The majestic character of the composition is complemented by the slight turning of the Madonna and Child toward the Magi, thus being an Epiphany, the first manifestation of the divinity of Christ. The arrangement of this composition of the Virgin and Child —sometimes below a series of arches acting as a sort of baldachin— next to the Magi, is encountered in works done earlier than the Cardet frontal, for example, the *Frontal from Avià* (XIII, 122). The presence of the Epiphany in some apses must not be forgotten. We have already seen one example in Santa Maria d'Àneu (III, 37) and also in Santa Maria of Taüll (VII, 102), although they resort to a centralised composition, more in accordance with the frame of the apsidal vaulting.

The *Frontal from Mosoll* **67** does away with the central area: the Virgin and Child are visibly dislodged from the centre. This resolution reveals a less ceremonious treatment, favouring a narrative account. Moreover, it presents the subject of the Dormition of the Virgin, which also appears in the aforementioned *Frontal from El Coll.* This subject has its origin in the Byzantine world (*koimesis)* and can often be seen associated with the Assumption of Mary.

Further on, in other sections of the guide, other aspects of iconography are treated. The chronological discourse is again taken up in the next section on mural painting.

61 *Virgin from Ger*

SECOND HALF OF THE 12th CENTURY

THE *VIRGIN FROM Ger* is one of the most outstanding works in the collection and one of the most significant of its kind in Catalan Romanesque art. It forms part of a series of images of the Virgin which evolved in the Pyrenees, especially in Cerdanya, and were widespread in the bishopric of Urgell. These included works as relevant as the Bastanist —missing since 1936— and the one from Ix (Hix, Cerdagne). The Virgin from the collection of Eric de Kolb (New York) must also be included in this group. The *Virgin from Ger* is a piece of great quality, as can be appreciated in the delicacy of Mary's facial features, and in the softly falling folds of her garments, where the modelling of the hollowed out shapes are compensated by the rounded ones.

The rigid and frontal composition tends towards symmetry and stresses the distance between Mary and the Holy Child. As is customary, the facial expressions are serene and hieratic. Mary appears as the Throne of Christ and as the Seat of Wisdom. Her apparel has a priestly quality, given that the chasuble-looking cloak enhances the role of Mary as a symbol of the Church. Both figures wear crowns, initially of wood, but later substituted by metal ones. The seat is armless, simple, and chest-like, far from the monumentalism of other examples.

Some old photographs show the figure of the Holy Child placed at one side and leaning slightly towards Mary, as a sign of a more direct relationship between them. Perhaps this artefact was adjusted to conform to a different conception of their relationship, may be in the Gothic period. This remodelling suggests one of the most interesting aspects of the piece: that of the history posterior to the period it was made, as has occurred in other instances (VII, 103; VIII, 113).

66 *Altar frontal from Cardet*

SECOND HALF OF THE 13th CENTURY

THIS FRONTAL, ATTRIBUTED to the Ribagorça Workshop (XIX), comes from the parish church of Santa Maria in Cardet, in the Boí Valley. The figure of the enthroned Virgin as the seat for the Infant Jesus, that is, as a Seat of Wisdom, surrounded by the Tetramorph, is in the centre of the composition. A crowned Virgin is often a characteristic of the 13th century. The crown is a symbol of royalty, and here it is adorned with fleur-de-lys, a symbol of chastity associated with the figure of Mary. On the sides, the infancy of Christ is told in an essentially narrative manner, beginning with the Annunciation and the Visitation in the upper left quadrant, followed by the Nativity and the Annunciation to the Shepherds in the upper right, where some features of a very stylized landscape can be observed. In the lower left, the story continues, depicting the three Magi of the Epiphany who are on their way to worship Jesus; and lastly, the Slaughter of the Holy Innocents and the Flight to Egypt. The Slaughter of the Holy Innocents is difficult to recognize because details of the painting have not been preserved, such as the spears and the murdered children. These details had been painted on the metal, and on the *colradura* that covered the stucco reliefs in the background. When the metal and varnish fell off, so did the painted details. The most recent restoration of the piece has revived and defined the original colours. The *Cardet Beam* (XIII, 126) comes from the same church; it is exhibited in Section XIII.

67 *Altar frontal from Mosoll*

MIDDLE OF THE 13th CENTURY

THE SCENES ON THE frontal, which are placed in apparent disorder, exalt the saving role of the Virgin, as the Mother of God associated with the Redemption. The joint figures of Jesus and Mary, variously superposed, occupy two of the central compartments. At either side, above and below, the Holy Infant is recognised as being the Messiah, both in the Adoration of the Magi, and in the greeting of Simon with his hands covered, during the Presentation in the Temple. This scene where Joseph offers the young pigeons, symbolising the purity of the Virgin, alludes to the redemptive sacrifice of Christ, as can be seen in the presence of the consecrated host on the altar. The angel's Annunciation to Mary, coinciding with the Incarnation, is the prelude to Redemption. In the Visitation, Elizabeth recognises the Mother of God. Lastly, we see the Dormition of Mary, a subject that will become important during the Gothic period; the presence of the Son blessing her is an affirmation of the extremely important function of the Mother.

Santa Maria in Mosoll, the church where the frontal is from, was profaned by the soldiers of the Viscount of Castellbó in the midst of the Albigensian rebellion, about 1197-98. It is most likely that the idea to paint the frontal came about during the restoration of the church.

SECTION V

The paintings from Sant Climent in Taüll. Liturgical furnishings in the Romanesque church

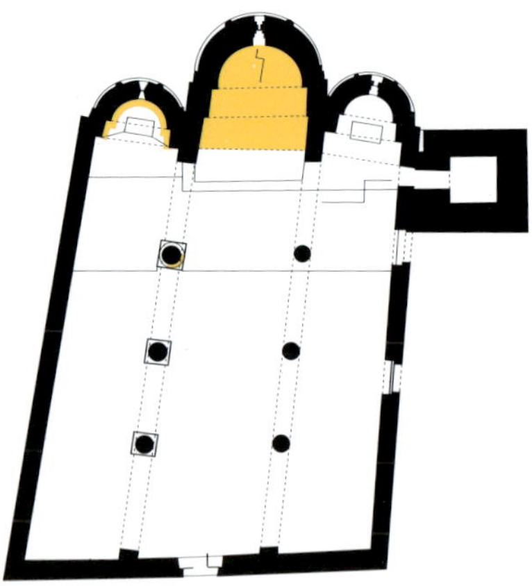

Paintings conserved in the MNAC

ONE OF THE MOST important groups of Catalan, as well as European, Romanesque wall paintings comes from the Church of Sant Climent in Taüll in the Boí Valley. Most of these paintings are conserved in the Museu Nacional d'Art de Catalunya, with a few of them remaining *in situ*. The decoration of the central apse (the vaulting and semicircular wall) is to be found in the MNAC, plus the decoration of the two triumphal arches and that from the north, or Gospel side, lateral apse.

Although many art historians have analysed the mural group from Sant Climent in Taüll, the definitive monographic study that it merits has yet to be published. It should be mentioned that very few stylistic analogies have been established to explain the origin of the painter who executed one of the most perfect works in Romanesque art. Moreover, the scant comparisons which have been made are controversial. On the whole, most historians coincide in admitting a Byzantine influence that perhaps could be explained by the

influence of painting from Lombardy. The background bands of colour where figures are inscribed, so common on Catalan wall painting, have been linked to Mozarab miniature. However, the monumental character of the figures enables a comparison to be made with the first workshops of the school of Toulousaine sculpture.

On the vaulting of the central apse the figure of Christ in Majesty is portrayed within the mandorla, seated on the arc of heaven, with the Earth as a footstool beneath His feet: a Theophany inspired in the Book of Revelation and other biblical sources, such as the visions of Isaiah, the Gospels of St. John and St. Matthew, and the Acts of the Apostles (Revelations 1, 7-8; 20, 11 & 21, 6; Isaiah 66, 1; John 1, 4-5; Matthew 5, 34-35; Revelations 7, 49). The mandorla around the *Maiestas* is set against a background of blue, ochre and black bands.

Christ is a solemn, majestic figure: His right hand is in a gesture of blessing; an open book in His left where the inscription '*EGO SUM LUX MUNDI*' ('I am the light of the world'; John 8, 12) can be seen. The light is interpreted as the Word, from the Greek *logos*: The Word bestows life and it is the beginning and end of everything. In the Book of Genesis, at the moment of Creation, light is opposed to

the darkness of night and evil. The Word is life, and life is the light of the world that shines in the darkness. The light is also the word of the Prophets which has illuminated the Apostles; it is the truth that reveals us the existance of God.

From the artistic and stylistic viewpoint, the drawing of Christ's hands, albeit stylised and simplified, reveals their anatomy. The facial features, framed by his long hair, are arranged in a perfect axial symmetry. The eyes are the focal point: they are impressive and magnificent. Christ wears a grey and white tunic and a blue cloak, the borders of which are shown incrusted with precious stones. The

folds of His garment, together with the use of glazes, form rich and elegant volumes, giving an illusion of movement.

On both sides of Christ, the letters Alpha and Omega, the first and last letters of the Greek alphabet, indicate that He is the Beginning and the End of all things (Revelations, 1, 8; 21, 6; 22, 13).

Outside the mandorla, the Tetramorph is found in an original and elaborate composition. Below, there are four circles which at times have been interpreted as Jehovah's chariot wheels. Two angels and the symbols of the

Evangelists Mark and Luke, the lion and the ox, appear within said circles. The other two symbols of the Tetramorph can be seen on the upper section, in the spaces between the mandorla and the front of the apse. To the right of Christ, the angel symbolizing Matthew is depicted, and paired on the other side, the figure of another angel, his hands covered in a sign of respect, holds the eagle symbolising John. Completing the composition are two seraphim, depicted with eyed wings, a sign of the Revelation.

In spite of the Italian influence on the apsidal paintings from Sant Climent in Taüll, Romanesque painting reaches here a state of conceptual speculation, abandoning any attempt to describe reality. This can be understood as the theorisation of the presence of the Divinity, the Theophany. Although the symbols in the work incorporate connotations of God as creator, as the beginning and the end of all things and as the judge in the Last Judgement, this depiction on the apse from Sant Climent in Taüll privileges the majestic vision of the Theophany; it is simply an image of divinity in itself. When M. Durliat was defining the synthetic vision of Sant Climent in Taüll, he said —referring to the art of visionaries and theologists— that they scorned narrative concerns and the desire to enlighten.

In the semicircular area, framed by arches and columns, several Apostles and Saints are portrayed in an iconographic arrangement which has precedents in the Coptic chapels of Baouit and Saqqare (5th and 6th centuries) that went on to have a widespread influence in Western art during the early Middle Ages. At both sides of the axial window, the Virgin and John the Evangelist appear, the latter displaying the book that inspires the vision or Theophany exhibited on the apsidal vaulting. Next to the Virgin, the Apostles Bartholomew and Thomas are depicted. James is next to John, but few traces are preserved of another Apostle, who may be Philip. The Virgin holds a patera that radiates light in her covered hand; this flat dish has a eucharistic, christological and ecclesial meaning. The headdress she wears, despite its geometric design, recalls the usual treatment given to this image in Byzantine painting, which has also been captured in the carving of the Virgin in the depictions of the Descents from the Cross from Durro, Erill and Taüll (VIII, 110-112). A complicated fret in perspective terminates this section of the mural at its lower edge.

The border of the arc on which the Lord is seated stands out from the other ornamental designs on the apse, as well as the edging on Christ's robes. The former has a well-defined plant motif, also found in other mural groups, for instance in the *Apse from Sant Pere in La Seu d'Urgell* (I, 1), Santa Maria in Barberà, Polinyà (Museu Diocesà in Barcelona), the atrium from Cardona (XIV) and in San Isidoro de León. This motif also can be seen on the portable altar of the Cathedral of Paderborn among other examples. As for architectural simulated forms, we will meet them again in Santa Maria in Taüll (VII) and in Maderuelo (Museo del Prado, Madrid).

On the first of the arches preceding the apse is the *Dextera Domini*, or the Hand of God, inscribed in a circle, in a gesture of blessing. On the side of the arch showing the Hand of God, the figure of Abel might be represented, the first among the Righteous and a precursor of Christ. On the keystone of the other arch, and forming a vertical axis in respect to the *Maiestas*, is the *Agnus Dei*, or Lamb of God, symbol of the death and resurrected Christ. Its seven eyes symbolize the plenitude and omniscience of Christ (Revelations 5, 6-14). On the intrados of this same arch, to the left, there are two scenes in square compartments. On the one above, only the lower part of two personages is preserved. The scene below represents the parable of the poor man, Lazarus, and the rich man, narrated in the Gospel of St. Luke (Luke 16, 19-31), which evokes the Salvation and the separation of the blessed and the damned at the Last Judgement. Another representation of the parable appears in a fragment from Sorpe that is conserved in the Museu Diocesà d'Urgell, and in the paintings in Saint-Martin de Vicq (Indre, France).

The current installation at the Museum has restituted five of the six angels that originally adorned the north apse. In previous museographical displays they had been displayed on a flat support. The sixth angel which was removed using a different technique, *stacco*, is exhibited on a separate panel. These angels, which have minor technical and artistic qualities when compared to the central apse, are the work of another painter, the one who probably did the Last Judgement mural in the Church of Santa Maria in Taüll (VII). The subject of choirs of angels is frequent in Romanesque painting; the Italian frescoes of Sant'Angelo in Formis and San Vincenzo al Volturno are good examples of this.

The panel showing a man meditating comes from the first triumphal arch of the central apse, but it is exhibited separately because the exact place where it was located is unknown. There have been many hypotheses on the identity of the man; most are in favour of either Job or Jacob. Similar figures appear in the triumphal arches from Ginestarre (IV, 46) and from Baltarga (Museu Diocesà d'Urgell).

On the panel to the left, the decoration on the intrados of a walled up window, was found in the lower part of the central apse, beneath the present paintings. Hence, the window and its decoration come from an earlier building.

As it has been said before, a definitive study on the style of the paintings on the central apse from Sant Climent still needs to be written. Only the chapel paintings of St. Augustine, in the old Cathedral of Roda d'Isábena in Huesca, are comparable in style and in quality to the ones from Sant Climent, but at present they are in an extremely poor state of preservation. They are also similar to the figures of the triumphal arch of the south apse of Santa Maria in Taüll. Moreover, the exceptional artistic qualities of the paintings from Sant Climent are in keeping with the conclusions of the study of the pigments, which are superior in quality and preparation than in other Catalan churches, and even include some imported pigments. The technique is also exceptional. The painter has achieved very intense chromatic effects by superimposing several layers of paint. Thus the blue, obtained from aerinite, has been applied over a layer of black, and as for the red, cinnabar is laid on top of haemitite, a ferrous oxide.

The church was consecrated on 10 December in 1123 by Bishop Ramon of Roda, who signs as Bishop of Barbastro. The inscription from the time of the consecration is painted on the first Gospel-side column (north): *'ANNO AB INCARNACIONAE / DOMINI M^{o}C^{o}XX°III° IIII° IDVS DECEMBRIS / VENIT RAIMUNDVS EPISCOPVS BARBASTRE / NSIS ET CONSECRAVIT HANC ECCLESIAM IN HONORE / SANCTI CLEMENTIS MARTIRIS ET PONENS RELI / QVIAS IN ALTARE SANCTI CORNELII EPISCOPI ET MARTIRIS'* ('The year of the Incarnation / of the Lord 1123, 10 December / came Ramon, Bishop of Barbastro / and consecrated this church in honour / of Saint Clement Martyr, and put relics / in the altar of Saint Cornelius, bishop and Martyr').

The epigraphic characters used for this inscription are identical to those on the paintings on the east end; this establishes the fact that they were done during the same period, and settle the dating to be during the episcopate of St. Ramon, Bishop of Roda and Barbastro, who had been the Prior of the Saint-Sernin community in Toulouse, Languedoc. Ample documentation exists about his activities, especially regarding the consecration of churches. He was Chaplain to the King of Aragon, Alfonso the Warrior, at the time that Barbastro, Daroca, Calatayud, Tudela and Zaragoza were conquered. The Lords of the Boí Valley, the Erill family, as well as the Counts of Pallars, took part in these campaigns and returned from them with wealth which they probably spent in the valley rebuilding and decorating several churches, including Sant Climent and Santa Maria in Taüll. This historical fact would explain and justify the presence of master craftsmen and workshops of a very high artistic level in the valley.

In addition to the wall paintings, this section exhibits a series of objects related to church furnishings during the Romanesque period; they are displayed in the area that evokes the side aisle of Sant Climent in Taüll. The essential element is the altar (see the altar stone in Section II), which is here represented by the example from Sant Romà de Vila (Andorra), **82** from which the side and central panels are preserved. It has been placed below a baldachin that reproduces a structure of a shrine with two original panels and a capital of unknown origin **81**. However it should be remembered that there are examples of a further typology, that of a panel supported by beams, such as the baldachins from Tost and Tavèrnoles, exhibited elsewere in the Museum (IV, 47 & XIII, 124). The presbyterial bench must also has been in a prominent place **70**.

The two showcases contain several objects for liturgical use. Some of them were placed on the altar: the cross is the most important element (72); the caskets used as reliquaries **75**; the candlesticks which were displayed in pairs (74); and the book, which was often luxuriously bound with decorated plates (79). There is also a lipsanothèque **71** or reliquary which was housed in a special compartment within the altar. Noteworthy among the sacred receptacles are the ciborium, (76) where the consecrated hosts were stored, and the pyx (77) where the hosts were stored before being consacrated. Another fundamental component of the liturgy is the censer, whose smoke is interpreted as a prayer to God **73**. The boats (78) in which the incense was stored are an essential adjunct to the censer.

At the end of this section, a holy water stoup is on view (80) along with the wrought-iron facings from a door (83). Both of these pieces are of unknown origin.

70 *Presbyterial bench from Sant Climent in Taüll*

12th OR 13th CENTURY

THIS BENCH IS a unique piece within the church furnishings of the time. It is characterised by its compartmentalized structure of three arches over columns and by its crest. The bench used to be attached to the floor. It is of a similar typology to certain choir stalls from the 13th to the 15th centuries found on the Iberian Peninsula (Astudillo, Gradefes). The fretwork is another striking feature of this bench. The motifs are varied but simple: they are mainly floral and geometrical designs (palmettes, arches, chequered patterns, etc.). And some of them belong to earlier traditions than the Romanesque, having a markedly popular appearance, as found in other pieces from the Pyrenees. The closest parallel is found in the Boí Valley, on two reused panels from the church in Durro.

The Taüll bench has been subject to modern restorations and transformations. This can be deduced from the metal reinforcements on the back and from some dovetailing elements. Moreover, it is very different from other furnishings more closely related to the major artistic tendencies, such as *Sant Ramon's Chair* from the Cathedral of Roda de Isábena (Huesca). Thus, it is difficult to tell the age of the bench, given that the decoration is so simple and popular.

71 *Lipsanothèque from Sant Climent in Taüll*

END OF THE 11th CENTURY

***LIPSANOTHÈQUES* OR VESSELS THAT WERE USED** as reliquaries and kept within the altar are another of the important objects of church furnishings. They are often made of wood and have the shape of a rectangular, oval or cylindrical box, or, as in this example from Taüll, are spherical in form. Here the decoration is arranged in horizontal bands with simple plant motifs, as in the case of the palmettes on the lid of this piece, and with other geometric or figurative patterns. In this instance, three fish are depicted, having a christological meaning related to the Eucharist, which is celebrated at the altar. This same motif appears on one of the lipsanothèques discovered in 1984 in the church of Sant Gregori in the area of Girona; it contained different relics wrapped in a cloth from the 11th or 12th century and a parchment from the time the church was consecrated in the 11th century. The fish motif also appears on a reliquary that is conserved in the Museu Episcopal de Vic.

73 *Censer*

FIRST HALF OF THE 12th CENTURY

THE TYPICAL ROMANESQUE CENSER, an object used during Mass and in other liturgical rites, consists of two joined pieces: the lower piece or cup, that was used to burn the aromatic resin, and the upper part or the cap, which has openwork to let out the smoke from the incense. In this piece, the four iron rods that held it, and the chains to support and swing it, are missing. This censer has a globular or spherical shape, customary during the 12th century, and different from the ones with architectural shapes alluding to celestial Jerusalem (XV). Despite its condition which shows a considerable loss of enamel and gilt, it is interesting because its decoration is designed in eight circles where pairs of facing birds are engraved, a device often used in the Romanesque and which recalls Oriental art, as in the *Islamic plaque* from Toledo (I, 21). It is very possible that this piece came from a local workshop, without this intending to minimise comparisons with works from Limoges. This, then, is a piece of enormous interest in that it reflects works done prior to the 13th-century enormous diffusion of products from Limoges.

75 *Châsse of St. Stephen*

C. 1210-20

THIS RELIQUARY CASKET is very representative of work done in Limoges, particularly because it is dedicated to St. Stephen, a martyr whose cult was very important in this city. On the front part of the casket, two key subjects from the life of the saint are illustrated: on the upper part, he is being led to his martyrdom, and on the lower, he is being stoned. In this scene, the saint appears between two executioners, and Saul, the future St. Paul, on the left, consents to the martyrdom of St. Stephen. The composition tends toward centralization, differing from the paintings from Sant Joan in Boí (II). Various arguments enable us to date this piece to the first decades of the 13th century. Firstly, the subject matter is related to martyred saints, a strong development in that period. Secondly, both the reserved treatment of the figures and the range of colours are considered characteristic of Limoges work at that time.

81 *The so-called Baldachin from Toses*

FIRST THIRD OF THE 13th CENTURY

THE BALDACHIN, OR ciborium, is the piece of furniture which has the function of providing a canopy for the altar, in order to give relevance to the most important place in the church. As we mentioned in the introduction to this section, the baldachin can assume two forms: as a panel to be tilted over the altar, as in the *Baldachin from Tost* (IV, 47) and the *Tavèrnoles baldachin* (XIII, 124); or it can take the form of a shrine on columns, as in the so-called *Baldachin from Toses.* It is not absolutely certain whether this baldachin comes from the church in Toses. It was reconstructed by J. Folch i Torres using the only two panels that had been preserved. He also used a Romanesque capital carved in wood of unknown provenance.

On the front spandrels of the baldachin, two prophets, Daniel and Jeremiah, are depicted. Their presence could be explained by the apocalyptic and messianic character of their prophecies. As far as the style is concerned, these figures show a dependence on the more elaborate models of the renewal in the year 1200 (XIII). On the interior face of the baldachin, a medall; oned bestiary is made up of depictions of real and mithological animals, and the signs of the zodiac. On both faces the chromatic contrast between red and dark-green is made much of.

82 *Altar from Sant Romà de Vila*

FIRST HALF OF THE 13th CENTURY

THIS ALTAR COMES FROM the Church of Sant Romà de Vila, in Andorra. The altar is the most important place in the church because it is where the sacrament of Holy Communion takes place. Sometimes, however, the altar was only covered with a simple cloth, although more sumptuous altar coverings were made using gold and silver. In others, as in Sant Romà de Vila, the altar was covered with painted panels. In this instance, the frontal and two side panels have been preserved; on the former, Christ in Majesty is portrayed surrounded by the Tetramorph and by the Apostles. The iconography on the right side panel catches the eye: this depicts the Assumption of the Virgin, who is being helped on her way to Heaven by angels. This theme became widespread during the Romanesque period thanks to the propagation of it feast day by the Abbot of Cluny, Peter the Venerable. The Assumption implies belief in the Resurrection of the corpse of the Virgin.

Stylistically speaking, this altar owes a debt to the great artistic renewal that took place *about* 1200 (XIII), although this particular work is somewhat irregular and rough in execution.

SECTION VI

Architectural sculpture

THIS SECTION IS a continuation of the series of sculptural work installed in Section I. Nevertheless, there are profound differences between the sculpture of the 11th century and the sculpture of the 12th and 13th centuries, as we shall now see. The pieces —almost all from Catalonia— enable us to see some of the most representative aspects of this art in the Romanesque period. The order in which they are presented is determined by the presence of two groups of sculptures of great size: the elements from the cloister of Sant Pere de les Puel·les **90** in Barcelona, and the ones from the east end of the church in Camarasa **92**. The way in which they are exhibited allows for a better understanding of the role sculpture played during the Romanesque period, and how this is a technique closely bound up with architecture, although subordinate to it.

Chiefly from *c.* 1100, sculpture contributed to the recovery of a feeling for modelling, and for volume, often stimulated by examples from Late Antiquity. This phenomenon was accompanied by the emergence of figuration —on doorways, windows, pillars and in other parts of buildings, such as the cloisters— and the development of programmes of images which could become quite extensive. A modest example is the Castilian double capital that contains scenes of the infancy of Christ (91). This change, however, seems to have occurred at a later date in Catalonia.

The selection and the ordering of the pieces also allow us to see a certain evolution in sculpture, and in some of its most significant characteristics. The first group of works consists of examples from the Pyrenees and northern Catalonia. Their forms and their repertoires of motifs introduce us to what we understand the Romanesque to be when speaking of architectural sculpture.

The first capitals show the tendency toward compositions based on geometric criteria (in accordance with its subordination to architecture as mentioned above), compositions which are governed by symmetrical patterns using both figurative subjects and floral designs. Thus, we can make sense of the

distortions and repetitions that the shapes of the figures are submitted to, as for instance on the capital decorated with upright griffins facing each other —their heads directed toward the upper corners of the piece **85**.

Furthermore, it is possible to observe different stylistic possibilities in this first group: the ones from the Ripoll workshops **84**; the ones from the workshops linked to Roussillon (86); and the ones from workshops related to the first two but associated with the Cathedral of La Seu d'Urgell, exemplified by in the cloister of Sant Serni de Tavèrnoles **89**.

Another capital can be related to this last group despite the use of different material: marble instead of granite (87). In general, all these centres maintained indirect links with Toulouse, although reminders of the Provençal world can also be found, as in the capitals of Santa Maria in Besalú **88**. The Corinthian capitals in this last group are examples of the use of classical patterns and floral motifs. The different versions are enormously varied and widespread, attaining extremely unequal levels of quality and approximation, some of which display greater ability (Camarasa), while others are much rougher. Some of these versions are often difficult to date (94 & 95).

Sant Pere de les Puel·les and Camarasa also take the lead in the series of works that are chronologically posterior. Almost all the specimens date from the 13th century and some of them are already at the threshold of the Gothic period. The shapes are more delicate, the volumes of the figures are more corporeal and have greater verisimilitude of gesture and the narrative quality of the scenes becomes more evident **97**.

The provenance of the sculptural groups in this series is from further south, although the group from Barcelona is notable for the number of pieces belonging to it. This can be explained by the fact that a great many of them had belonged to the Museo Provincial de Antigüedades in Barcelona, a museum consisting almost entirely of elements recovered from demolitions, building works and excavations carried out in that city between the 19th century and the beginning of the 20th. Other pieces enable us to directly relate various sculptural groups from Barcelona to that from Camarasa, since they share the same style and repertoire of plant motifs (93).

Among the more advanced works, the group from the Convent of Sant Francesc **96** is the most notable. It has been linked to one of the main Hispanic workshops producing sculpture at the end of the Romanesque age, that of the Master Mateo, related to the Pórtico de la Gloria of the Cathedral of Santiago de Compostela.

Furthermore, the continuity of influence of the Toulouse workshops during much of the 13th century is also suggested. The presence of motifs such as interlacing, scrolls and bands on which figurative elements are usually inscribed, shows the relationship between sculpture from Catalonia and Toulouse. This connection is specially obvious in the stonework of the Cathedrals of Lleida and Tarragona **98** & (99).

The last two pieces have more stereotyped forms, with a tendency to use simple and stylised floral motifs which anticipate the mass production that took place in the Gothic period (100 & 101). In this respect, it should be noted that the capital from Breda has a noticeable resemblance to some pieces in the cloister in Arles (Arles-sur-Tech, Vallespir) which is already considered to be Gothic.

84 *Voussoir from Ripoll*

SECOND HALF OF THE 12th CENTURY

THE FIRST PIECE in this section is an important example of the enormous production of the ateliers that worked on the Abbey of Santa Maria in Ripoll. This voussoir was found buried there by Antoni Coll i Fort, and because of its typology we can conclude that it was part of the arch over a doorway of said group. The piece is decorated with a human, and at the same time, monstrous head wearing a helmet, and in an attitude more of vomiting-up than of devouring the ram which emerges from its maw. Although it is difficult to interpret its symbolism, the negative meaning of the head is obvious; the monstrous features give it an undeniably demoniacal quality.

Stylistically, its descriptive character is striking. This is shown in the careful handling of the details: the precision, its relative geometricisation and the minute emphasis on the ferocious and monstrous aspects of the head. Taken as a whole, all these characteristics suggest that it is close in style to other works from Ripoll, among which the portal, part of the cloister of the Monastery of Ripoll, and other groups showing the same influence, such as the remains from the Cathedral of Vic, are of note. In general, these workshops exemplify the influence arriving from Languedoc. These analogies permit the dating of the relief as being from the second half of the 12th century.

85 *Capital*

END OF THE 12th CENTURY

THIS CAPITAL, which is decorated on all four sides, displays one of the most common decorative designs in Romanesque figurative sculpture, the symmetrical arrangement of pairs of animals or grotesque creatures. In this case, there are griffins facing each other on all four sides of the capital. Their heads are oriented toward the angles, and they are biting their own wings. The subject and the composition are habitual, especially in the larger centres of production in the north of Catalonia, in the eastern part of the Catalan Pyrenees. In that respect, they bring the output of the Roussillon workshops to mind, as exemplified in the tribune at Serrabona (Serrabone, Roussillon), whose repertoire of designs was widespread in the Empurdà and Girona area, from where this capital probably comes.

88 *Capitals from Besalú*

BETWEEN 1137 AND 1167/71

THESE FIVE CAPITALS of embedded columns are a clear example of the way architectural sculpture was put to use in the 12th century. They come from one of the three important Besalú groups: the Church of Santa Maria, in particular from the building work done when adapting the edifice to the requirements of the congregation of Saint-Ruf d'Avignon between 1137 and the years 1167/71. Nevertheless, it is possible that the work went on until 1185, when Pere, the Prior of Santa Maria, received the right —from the Count and King, Alfons I the Chaste— to extract stone from within the boundaries of Besalú. Other pieces from the same group can be seen in Barcelona in the building known as the Conventet, opposite the Monastery of Pedralbes.

The group is divided into two series according to their subject matter and their original location. The subject matter closely follows that of Antiquity, given the more or less faithful use of compositional schemes and motifs from Corinthian capitals. The deeply etched and vigorous carving, combined with the generous use of trepanning, is related to the sculpture of the Mediterranean Languedoc area and the region of Provence. These regions, where the classical influence was still strong, had a great influence on many of the workshops active in Catalonia during the Romanesque period. To be more specific, the major reference may have been the austere sculpture of Saint-Ruf d'Avignon, a canonical abbey on which Santa Maria in Besalú was dependent. However, this does not mean that there was direct contact among the workshops.

The two remaining capitals come from apsidal exteriors. Their compositions consist of figures grasping the stems of the volutes, flanked by birds, in all likelihood eagles. The rough carving, which coincides with that of the small heads on the Corinthian capitals, indicates that the workshop was not used to figuration.

89 *Capitals from Tavèrnoles*

SECOND HALF OF THE 12th CENTURY

THERE ARE STILL remains *in situ* of the south church cloister of the Benedictine Monastery of Sant Serni de Tavèrnoles. The capitals exhibited here come from this cloister and are directly linked to the workshops of the Cathedral of La Seu d'Urgell. Account must be taken of the fact that this cathedral constitutes one of the great constructional undertakings of the second half of the 12th century in the Pyrenees, and that it has points of contact with works from the regions of the Ripollès, Roussillon, and also Toulouse in Languedoc.

Granite, a material frequently used in this part of the country, gives the capitals from Tavèrnoles a robust appearance, with a predominance of smooth and barely detailed surfaces. On the other hand, the relief work as a whole is noteworthy for the clarity of volume and composition, the latter characterised, as is customary, by its symmetry.

One of the most significant themes is that of figures who emerge from behind clusters of leaves. This motif, which appears in two of the capitals from Tavèrnoles and in another capital from this same section (87), was very frequent in the Romanesque period. There also are zoömorphic figures, such as the birds placed on the angles of a capital, in addition to floral motifs of a Corinthian type. The sixth capital from this group, which is not exhibited, has a much simpler design (MNAC/MAC 24006).

90 *Fragments of the cloister of Sant Pere de les Puel·les*

AFTER 1187

THE CLOISTER OF THE Monastery of Sant Pere de les Puel·les in Barcelona was torn down in 1873 along with the monastic outbuildings, abandoned since 1835. Numerous pieces were dispersed in various collections, and some went into the Museo Provincial de Antigüedades. The montage exhibited here is the result of the museographic presentation in 1934. It consists of three arches constructed from diverse typological elements which come from those remains, and is completed by various added elements.

This group is an example of the art produced in Barcelona between the end of the 12th century and the beginning of the 13th. The appearance of the cloister, evoked here by the reconstructed arcade, can be deduced from drawings made before and after its demolition. The traces of polycromy are from a later period than the building of the cloister.

Despite its robustness, this style has been connected to the workshops active in Barcelona, especially in the 13th century. These workshops produced important groups, such as the cloister doorway of the Cathedral, and the cloister of Sant Pau del Camp. In fact, some of the pieces which are conserved in other collections allow the ones from Sant Pere de les Puel·les to be linked to more important ensembles. A dating reference is 1187, when Beatriu of Rocafort pledged to have a cloister built in front of the door of the refectory.

92 *Ensemble from Camarasa*

FIRST THIRD OF THE 13th CENTURY

THIS ENSEMBLE OF pieces comes from the Church of Sant Miquel, at the Camarasa Castle, and is one of the most important examples in the Museum as far as Romanesque architectural sculpture is concerned. As old photographs show, the group comes from the apse and transept of the building, where an important part of the sculpted decoration is still preserved.

Among the objects conserved in the Museum, the most splendid is a pillar from the transept. This pillar combines the Corinthian capital with historiated items. On the left is the scene of Original Sin: Adam and Eve are to either side of the tree around which the serpent, a symbol of the devil, is wound. This theme represents the Fall of man. On the right, we see a depiction of Isaac's sacrifice, which foreshadows the death of Christ. At the same time this scene is an allusion to the Eucharist, held at the altar, and for this reason it often appears near the chancel. Furthermore, according to a recent thinking, the proximity of both scenes in Camarasa may also respond to the wish to underline the contrast between the disobedience of Adam and Eve and the obedience of Abraham.

To the right of the pillar, there are four of the capitals that come from the interior of the apsidal windows, and another that was located outside. The plant forms of the decoration are characterised by the delicate and supple shapes, a taste for detail and the clear-cut relief work.

The style and the repertory of designs make it possible to link the group with diverse monuments in Barcelona **(93)**: the Church of Sant Martí Sarroca — where important architectural analogies can be observed— and the cloister of Sant Benet de Bages. Together with the pieces from Barcelona, the value of the Camarasa group resides in the fact of demonstrating the contacts existing between all these groups during the first third of the 13th century.

96 *Capitals from the Convent of Sant Francesc*

C. 1200-20

ALONG WITH THE GROUP of pieces from Camarasa, this is the most important group from the beginning of the 13th century, and without doubt, one of the most noteworthy in the exhibition. These marble capitals were discovered during excavations made for the building of a house in the Duc de Medinaceli square in Barcelona. They have always been linked to the cloister of Sant Nicolau, a pilgrims' hospital where the Convent of Sant Francesc was later built in 1232. Neither building exists today.

The first capital (MNAC/MAC 14202), a corner capital, exhibits figures emerging from among acanthus leaves, a very widespread motif that can be seen on other capitals in this same section (87 & 89). The agility of forms and volumes —having a certain classicising air, above all in the heads— is of note. The second capital (MNAC/MAC 14203), decorated on three of its sides, depicts a procession of monks, each holding liturgical objects. The third (MNAC/MAC 12206), which is quite mutilated, is decorated with plant motifs.

At present, it is impossible to tell what the original function of these pieces was. Apart from their relationship to the cloister mentioned above, it has also been suggested that these capitals may have had a function in a funerary context, perhaps as part of a tomb.

Stylistically, these pieces are an example of an art closer to the Gothic period. They are related to the work from the milieu of Master Mateo, from the Pórtico de la Gloria of the Cathedral of Santiago de Compostela. Thus, the principal merit of the capitals stems from being a noteworthy reflection in Catalonia —particularly in Barcelona— of work done in the north-west of Spain during the first few decades of the 13th century.

97 *Capital*

FIRST QUARTER OF THE 13th CENTURY

THIS CAPITAL HAS OFTEN BEEN linked to the group mentioned above (96), but it can be judged separately. This piece is carved on all four sides. On one side we see two figures: a king and a lady —perhaps his wife— on horseback; in the centre, another figure points to the king. On the other sides, there are figures in postures denoting sorrow and despair, perhaps as part of a funerary iconography. Although some irregularities can be observed in the organisation of the composition, such as the disproportionate smallness of the horses' hooves, the style of the relic is associated with works produced in Catalonia between the end of the 12th century and the early decades of the 13th on account of the full shapes that are compressed into the available space. These works, and the ones in the Cathedrals of Lleida and Tarragona, are linked to centres in Languedoc and Provence.

98 *Capital*

SECOND THIRD OF THE 12th CENTURY

THIS CAPITAL IS one of few non-Catalan works in this section. The piece exemplifies another typical theme of the Romanesque period: the interlacing of plant motifs based on stems and palmettes. But above all, it represents one of the most creative and widespread schools of 12th-century sculpture: the school of Toulouse. Thus, similar plant motifs have been found on pieces from the cloisters of Saint-Sernin and the Cathedral of Saint-Étienne in Toulouse (Languedoc), as well as in places that directly show its influence. In spite of its deterioration, this type of relief is also noteworthy, having two planes visible through the openwork, as in Saint-Sernin. It is logical, then, to locate the origin of this capital to the south of France, somewhere between Languedoc and Gascogne.

SECTION VII

The paintings from the Church of Santa Maria in Taüll

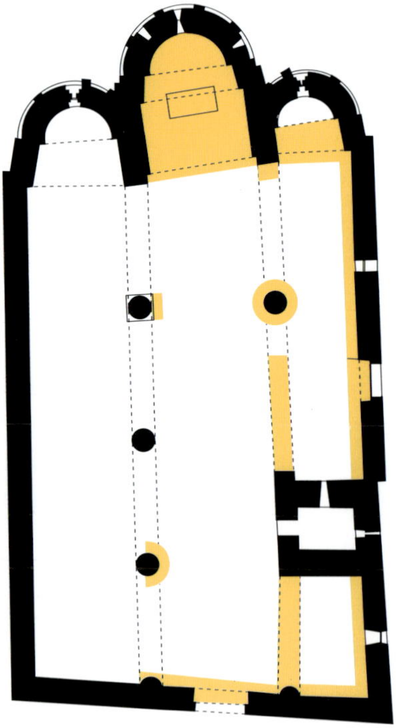

Paintings conserved in the MNAC

AFTER THE SECTION ON SCULPTURE, the visitor again finds him or herself in the Boí Valley, in the second of the churches of Taüll, Santa Maria, the parish church of the village of Taüll. Conserved here is a remarkable set of paintings from that church —two-thirds of whose architecture has been reproduced— and these form the most complete group in the Museum. The present installation attempts to grant them more prominence by providing an overall view from the raised entrance to the section. In addition to the paintings displayed in earlier installations, fragments never before seen have been incorporated which help to complete the ensemble and demonstrate its complexity.

The paintings can be broken down into three groups, due not only to their original location but for reasons of iconography and style. The first group consists of paintings from the central apse and the two arches that lead up to it; the second group consists of the paintings that used to give onto the south apse —now reconstructed; and lastly, the

paintings from the rest of the church; namely, from the west and south walls, the intradoses of the arches, and the columns. We shall treat these three groups of paintings in the same order as they are mentioned above.

The paintings on the main apse, which historiography attributes to the Master of Santa Maria, are not only notable for their remarkable quality, their iconography and their varied polychromy, but also for the richness and variety of their decorative themes.

On the apse vaulting, the Epiphany, the first acknowledgement of Christ's divinity, is depicted. Mary is at the centre of the vaulting in an attitude at once hieratic and majestic; she is the Seat of Wisdom, that is, of the Word incarnate. On the either side are the Three Wise Men offering their gifts to the Christ Child: Melchior is on the left, and Gaspar and Balthazar are on the right. The star *('STELA')* that has guided them to the Child appears twice on the vault of heaven; this fact has been interpreted as an allusion to the two testaments, the Old and the New Law. According to the biblical texts, the Magi are sages from the East

(Matthew 2, 1-12), representing all the nations of the Earth as well as the three stages in the life of man. The subject of the Epiphany has always been very popular in Christian culture; it has often been treated in liturgical drama, such as in the *Officium Stellae*, which was widely performed in the 11th and 12th centuries. Although the scene of the Adoration of the Magi dates to the origins of Christian iconography, a certain stiffness in the figure of Mary and her seat of honour suggests that a carved or cast image of the kind used in performances of said liturgical drama might have been used as a model for this scene.

The sequence of images continues with the paintings on the vaulting of the two arches preceding the apse. On the nearest arch to the latter is the Lamb of God, symbol of the dead and resurrected Christ, which looks toward the right. Blessed by the *Dextera Domini,* the right hand of God, Abel makes his offering; he appears near the altar of the apse because he is both prefiguration and allegory of Christ's sacrifice and the Eucharist. On the vaulting of the other arch the rare traces of painting that have been preserved suggest that originally the figure of the *Maiestas Domini* was placed here, within a mandorla supported by angels whose remains can still be seen. The Tetramorph, seraphim and archangels were on the lateral intradoses of the arch. The intrados on the right, the only one preserved, is remarkable and shows a great similarity to a representation on the apse of Santa Cruz de Maderuelo (Museo del Prado). It includes four figures: two anthropozoömorphic depictions of the Evangelists Mark and John on either side of a seraph, and in the right-hand corner, the Archangel Gabriel.

On the semicircular part below these Theophanic portrayals, and framed by a series of arches, are the Apostles, witnesses to the divine manifestation, with Peter and Paul, pillars of the Church, in the centre. The space allocated to the Apostles spreads to the two pre-apsidal arches, where there are only a few remaining traces of paint. However, the fact that there is enough room for more than twelve figures allows us to supose that, as well as the Apostles, there may been other saints depicted.

On the lower part of the apse and on the two arches in front of it, there is a frieze of medallions in which real and imaginary animals, perhaps inspired by Oriental textiles, are inscribed. The medallions are repeated on the drapery below. And on the altar, situated in the exact place it occupied in the original apse, a subject inspired by them is visible: tangential circles within which animals were inscribed, although their composition is rather rudimentary and irregular.

Only the decoration of the triumphal arch and upper wall of the extrados has been preserved from the south apse, which was pulled down to build a new sacristy. The paintings on the window recess come from the north apse. The paintings are of a very high quality, especially the ones on the triumphal arch which are being exhibited here for the first time. On the keystone is the hand of God extended toward the people and contained in a shield or *clipeus*, which is held by two splendidly painted, although rather badly preserved, angels. Lower down, beneath a lintel supported on capitals, there are two saints, one on each side. The face of the one on the right, which is better preserved, shows both a serene beauty and great strength, comparable to the ones on the apse of Sant Climent in Taüll. On the wall above the apse appear two peacocks ('*PAVO*') drinking from a chalice, like the Christian who drinks from the chalice of salvation, a subject from early Christianity repertoires.

All these paintings on the east end can be dated from the day the church was consecrated by Ramon, the Bishop of Roda and Barbastro, on 11 December 1123, the day after the consecration of the Church of Sant Climent.

The other paintings from the church —those on the perimetral walls, the columns and the intradoses— display a very homogeneous style and they are much more rudimentary than the ones on the east end of the church; they most likely come from a later period. In fact, when the paintings were removed from the south wall, a consecratory cross was found painted on the stonework. This proved, therefore, that the paintings on this wall were done after the consecration. Beginning with the Last Judgement portrayed on the west wall, all these paintings are attributed to another painter, called by historiography the Master of the Last Judgement. The output from the workshop of the Master of the Last Judgement lacks the monumentality and richness of colour of the work on the east end, although it does present interesting iconographic idiosyncracies, some of which are difficult to interpret. The decoration from the north apsidiole of Sant Climent in Taüll is also attributed to this painter. In addition, he is also linked to the decoration on the apse in Surp (XI, 118) as well as works from Aragon: the *Frontal from Vió* and the paintings from Susín, near Jaca.

The decoration of the south wall, on the part that extends from the belfry to the apse, contains two figurative bands that do not seem to be related to each other. The lower one —that should be looked at from right to left— begins with the angel's revelation to Zachariah of the birth of John the Baptist while Zachariah (partially obliterated) was officiating in the temple (Luke 1, 5-20). The narration continues as far as the other side of the portal, in the intrados of which there is another fragment, which has recently been added for the first time, of two fish facing a cross. The next scene is of the Naming of John the Baptist (Luke 1, 62-64), the Precursor. Following this, there comes Mary and the Holy Infant worshipped by the Three Wise Men, who are simultaneously visiting Herod, the first figure on the left. Among the scenes in the upper band, which are difficult to identify and do not seem to have any relationship with each other, a few warring angels can be discerned next to the belfry. This incomplete episode may be the battle of Michael and his angels against the dragon (Revelations 12, 7).

On the intradoses of the arches that separate the nave and the side aisles, saints and prophets are depicted. Opposite the south doorway —the one with the Lamb of God on the keystone— we can see a saint with a closed and sealed book, perhaps John the Evangelist. On the intrados of the arch nearest the west wall, Isaiah and Jeremiah appear. Their names are written backward, from right to left, which indicates that the painter was probably illiterate.

The columns were also decorated: the ones abutting onto the wall with borders and stripes, and the freestanding ones with saints and prophets. Two of the latter have been incorporated in the exhibit for the first time. They depict a number of saints as if they were pillars of the house of God. Nicolas is on the south column and Clement on the north-west column, at the bottom of the access stairs; both are tonsured and wearing celebrant dress and giving a blessing with the right hand. On this last column there are some graffiti, some of them not much later than the paintings, and related to the subject of the Last Judgement which is depicted nearby, as we shall see shortly. Thus, a maze with a cross in the centre would represent the difficult road to salvation that men must follow, and below, the Solomon's knot would allude to the

bonds of death as in the psalm (18 [17]) that is sung in the introit of the mass on Septuagesima Sunday at the beginning of the Easter cycle.

On the west wall of Santa Maria, an extremely original representation of the Last Judgement can be seen, as we have mentioned before. The central part is missing: it probably contained the figure of Christ in Majesty, come to judge the living and the dead, or perhaps the vacant seat of honour from which Christ is to judge them (or *Etimasia*). A number of beatified angels move towards the seat of honour, one of them carrying the cross, a symbol of the Resurrection which always appears in the depictions of the Last Judgement in Western art. On either side of the arch, St. Michael with a pair of scales in the scene in which souls are weighed, called Psychostasis, and on the right, souls burning in the fire of Purgatory or the gates of Hell. However, Hell is on the other side, on the south wall, in the chapel that is between the belfry and the west façade. There we see grotesque beings who torment the naked souls of the damned. At its side, on the west wall, but separated from the Last Judgement by a column, we see a version of the struggle between David and Goliath (1 Samuel 17, 4-54), which represents the struggle between good and evil. The angels below, who recall the ones from the north apsidiole of Sant Climent in Taüll, have been added to the exhibit for the first time, as has the figure holding a chalice on the belfry wall of this same chapel.

It seems as if only the paintings on the east end can be associated with the consecration in the year 1123, as we have mentioned before. Highly qualified and experienced artists from the workshop of Santa Maria in Taüll (the main apse) and from the workshop of Sant Climent (the south apse), would have had to work simultaneously, or with only a few years' difference to give expression to a programme of such great splendour and monumentality, so elaborate and coherent that it is considered among the best works of Romanesque painting in Catalonia. The rest of the paintings from the church show less artistic quality but they are extremely interesting for their iconography. They are attributed to a third workshop, that of the Master of the Last Judgement who would have been working a few years after the consecration of the church.

As far as painting technique and pictorial materials are concerned, the ones on the central apse stand out because of the intensity and variety of the colours, as well as the transparency of certain of the latter. Nonetheless, the colours employed are all made from natural earth pigments found in the Pyrenees. Their excellence stems from the way they were used and their colour combinations. On the paintings of the perimetral walls, the range of colours is more limited, and the painting technique is not so refined.

Also exhibited in the church are two examples of religious imagery which also come from Santa Maria: a crucified Christ **(104)** and a frontal with applied carved figures **103** that was doubtless part of a side altar.

103 *Altar frontal from Santa Maria in Taüll*

SECOND HALF OF THE 12th CENTURY
(REPAINTED IN 1579)

THE FRONTALS THAT have applied wood-carvings are an important variety in themselves, as are those painted directly onto panels which we have seen throughout the tour, and also the few preserved examples of fresco paintings, as is the case with the altar from Santa Maria in Taüll **(102.1)**.

This frontal, discovered during the expedition organised by the Institut d'Estudis Catalans in 1907, comes from a side altar in that church, and is one of the most significant examples of the technique of applied wood-carving. The *Christ from Basarán* —which we have already seen **(IV, 54)**— must also have formed part of one of these carved frontals. In Catalonia there are other important examples, such as the *Frontal from Sant Pere in Ripoll* (Museu Episcopal de Vic).

The frontals from Sant Pere in Ripoll, and from Taüll, follow almost the same compositional and iconographical scheme that we have seen before in various painted frontals: Christ in Majesty in the centre surrounded by the Tetramorph, and the Apostles in the lateral bands.

Stylistically, this frontal is thought to be related to other works from the region of Ribagorça. The figure of Christ is carved very carefully, especially his attire with its profuse overlapping geometricising folds, an element that suggests a later date within the second half of the 12th century.

This frontal is an example of the subsequent transformations undergone by certain Romanesque works, thus altering their initial appearance. In 1579 it was repainted, as it says on the inscription. It is also possible that a St. John from a calvary was added in the space that is now vacant. There is also documentary evidence of a restoration that took place in 1924 under Arturo Cividini.

SECTION VIII

Religious imagery

THE IMAGES CARVED in wood are one of basic elements in a church; they are usually placed near the altar. In this section of the exhibit we shall see a series of examples organised by typologies (from left to right: the Virgin and Holy Infant, the Descent from the Cross, and the Crucifix), which will allow us to analyse different aspects, such as their purpose, or the workshops where they were made. Nevertheless, some other important pieces have already been approached from the iconographic point of view (IV).

Catalonia is especially rich in these kinds of objects, at least as far as the quantity of works that have been conserved. On the whole, they are related to the typology and iconography prevailing in Europe at the time, although the existence of sumptuous pieces covered with precious metals and jewels should not be disregarded. The reliquary-image from Sainte-Foy-de-Conques, a well-known centre of pilgrimage, is of considerable interest, even though it dates from an earlier period and was re-elaborated at different times. Apart from certain documented and since-lost groups, there exist in Catalonia wood-carvings covered in tin (Tuir, Plandogau). Their design is identical to other images from the central France, which have been linked to the pilgrimage routes stemming from the cult of Mary. Furthermore, some pieces were made of stone, as were some altar frontals and other church furnishings. Links between examples of work in wood and stone have also been observed. In that sense, we should bear in mind the earlier comments on the image of the Virgin (IV, 63), related to the *Virgin of the Solsona Cloister.*

The images were located in special places, often on the altar. Some were characterised by their portable nature, given that they were used in liturgical ceremonies. Thus, the figures of the Virgin could be used in processions, a custom that has survived in some places. We have also alluded to their possible relation to liturgical theatre performed during the festivity of the Epiphany.

On the other hand, the carvings could be used as reliquaries. For this reason, some of them have a *reconditorio*, that is, a cavity where relics and documents of their consecration were deposited, as has been verified in some cases. One of the most outstanding examples is the *Christ from 1147* 113, an exceptional piece because its date of manufacture is known, unlike the immense majority of works of this kind. Other carvings that can be dated are the *Virgin from Sant Cugat del Vallès* (*c.* 1218), and a work already in the spirit of the Gothic period, the *Descent of Sant Joan de les Abadesses* (1251); neither of these are in the Museum. These are valuable chronological references, although it continues to be difficult to date these types of pieces with precision.

Wood sculpture was produced in workshops whose locations are unknown to us, although some of them —the ones dedicated to panel painting and writing-desks where manuscripts were worked on— were probably near to important monastic and cathedral centres. Stylistic analogies comprise the principal argument used to delimit the different groups. Such reasoning was used to define the so-called

Batlló Majesty

workshops of Ripoll, Urgell and Erill, mentioned by many scholars in their efforts to establish a classification of these works. On other occasions, however, the popular aspect of certain pieces **108** makes it difficult, or even prevents, their classification and dating. Lastly, many pieces which are the object of a devotional practice that has subsisted since the Middle Ages have suffered modification and restoration which has altered this original appearance.

The types of images are very easy to classify. The most widespread are the Virgin and the Crucifix. In addition, an important group of Descents from the Cross are conserved in Catalonia, as well as examples of Calvaries (IV, 53) and images of saints. Some pieces are integrated in groups combining differing techniques, such as the aedicule from Sant Martí d'Envalls in Angostrina (Angoustrine, Cerdagne), where we can also see scenes painted on a flat support. Two figures from Sant Martí Sarroca (Alt Penedès; MNAC/MAC 15924-15925) are conserved in the Museum, but are not exhibited. They may have formed part of one of these groups, as did an image of the Virgin which disappeared in 1936.

The tour through this section begins with a series of pieces from the typology called Virgin and Child, which come from diverse periods and places. The compositional scheme of the works is usually based on a rigid and almost symmetrical arrangement of the figure of Mary seated on a chair which is generally in the shape of a throne, with the Christ Child seated in the centre or leaning slightly towards one side, almost always to the left (106 & 107). Among the works selected, there is a piece that dates from about the year 1200 and comes from Castile or Aragon (106). A similar date could be proposed for a Catalan piece **105**, and for the *Virgin from All* in Cerdanya (107), although the latter belongs to a different type, characterised, as has been said, by its monumentality. The *Virgin from Covet* **108** highlights the widespread appearance of this type, the popularity of some models, and the continuing use of these designs in the Gothic period. The fifth Virgin (109) exhibited in this space also corresponds to a later date.

Although they are located at the end of this section, we will comment on the crucifix carvings before we mention the Descents from the Cross because they allude to one of the key moments in the Redemption of humanity. They are the *Batlló Majesty* **114** and the *Christ from 1147* **113**, two of the most remarkable pieces in the Gallery. They belong to two of the more developed sets of conventions: the triumphant Christ and the suffering Christ respectively, which we will later analyse in detail.

The carvings which depict the Descent from the Cross are characteristic elements in the collection, and form an essential part of the group of works associated with the so-called Erill Workshop. The most significant place of provenance is the Boí Valley, where the exhibited works were originally from. Other examples have been added to the group, however, such as the *Christ from Mig-Aran*, that also formed part of a Descent from the Cross. The most important piece is the one that comes from Erill-la-Vall **111**. Alongside it, the *Virgin of the Descent from Durro* (110) enables us to observe the adaptation of the same composition of the figure of the Virgin at a greater scale by recourse to two pieces of wood. On the other hand, the figures belonging to the group from Santa Maria in Taüll **112** are thought to have been carved later.

Some of the basic elements of the Descents from the Cross that are exhibited in this section derive from the subject of the Crucifixion. Jesus Christ is in the centre of the composition, held up by Joseph of Arimathea on his right. Nicodemus, on his left, removes the nails. On either side, and almost symmetrically, are Mary and St. John, with the thieves at either end. Some of the details in Catalan carvings are exceptional, above all the figures of the two thieves, Dymas and Gestas. The inclusion of the two thieves contrasts with representations of the same subjects in other locations, where they are not depicted. Some of the figures have a peg protruding from their feet, which was inserted into a beam above the altar. However, such figures could also be placed near the entrance to the church.

The development of the subject of the Descent from the Cross in the Romanesque period, associated at times to liturgical theatre, provides a more narrative and dramatic sense to the treatment of the Calvary episodes. As some have tried to demonstrate, the relative importance of these statuary groups in Catalan art of the 12th and 13th centuries —for example, the *'Santíssim Misteri' in Sant Joan de les Abadesses*— might have to do with the fight against the spread of Catharism. Some treatise-writers, such as Amalarius of Metz, Bishop of Treves in Carolingian times, gave a eucharistic meaning to this subject, and to some of its characters. Later, this idea could have been used as a response to the denial of the death of Christ, and even of the Eucharist, by the Cathars.

105 *Virgin*

C. 1200

THE RIGID AND FRONTAL composition the piece depicts Mary as a throne for Christ, as in the examples from Ger and Matadars **(IV, 61 & 64)**. It retains some traces of its original polychromy, and of the first coat of whitish primer. Beneath the latter, some fragments of cloth are visible on Mary's right shoulder; these fragments were often applied in order to prevent movement of the wood.

As to particular attributes of the figure, Mary holds a spherical object in her right hand, possibly an apple. This fruit would allude to Eve, thus presenting Mary as the redeemer of Eve's sin. However, it can also be interpreted as a sphere, a symbol of power. Jesus is shown in his most customary pose, bestowing a blessing with His right hand and holding the book in His left. Furthermore, the crowns they both wear evoke their royal status. As in other examples, the back of the throne has a series of red and ochre bands, possibly heraldic in meaning. The composition and detailing, then, follow the conventions of the period, as do the adjacent pieces which come from other locations and are carved in very different styles **(106 & 107)**.

108 *Virgin from Covet*

13th CENTURY

THIS VIRGIN AND CHILD comes from the church in Covet and is characterised by the roughness of the handling. It preserves the rigid, frontal composition and customary attributes of this type of image. However, in this example the shapes are cruder, with less volume and greater irregularity (note the detail of Mary's hand, holding the Christ Child). The facial features are more down-to-earth, with a slight smile which reveals a certain, albeit unsuccessful, naturalist intent.

The *Virgin from Covet* thus represents a popular kind of production which, as its characteristics show, should not be necessarily included within the Romanesque canon. The piece demonstrates up to what point this type of image departs from the most prevailing tendencies, making it difficult to classify it both stylistically and chronologically. In any case, its similarity to other examples from the area around Lleida dating from the 13th century, as is the case with the one from Sant Cristòfol del Puig de

111 *Virgin and St. John of the Erill-la-Vall Descent from the Cross*

12th CENTURY

Meià (Noguera), has been noted.

THESE PIECES COME FROM the Church of Santa Eulàlia in Erill-la-Vall, in the Boí Valley: some are in the MNAC and others are in the Museu Episcopal de Vic. They are the most complete and representative group depicting the subject of the Descent from the Cross made in the so-called Erill Workshop, and they provide one of the most significant examples of medieval religious imagery in Catalonia. The seven figures that belong to this group were discovered in the porch of the church during the expedition of the Institut d'Estudis Catalans in 1907. Their composition and their postures coincide with the characteristics of the Catalan Descents from the Cross that we have already been mentioned.

The two pieces in the Museum are distinguished by their sense of volume, and by the delicacy of the features of the overall design and of the attire, which emphasises the anatomy of the figures and makes much of the subtle curves of the folds. The apparently severe facial features are in spirit of Far-Eastern art. However, analysis of the other pieces that belong to this group, currently in Vic, also denote more rigid and simplified forms, especially in the instance of the thieves.

Mary's head tilts slightly towards the centre of the composition, and stands out by her headdress. The latter has been considered a characteristic of the groups from the Boí Valley, and it has been linked to the figure of Mary on the apse of Sant Climent in Taüll (V). Apparently, Mary held Christ's right arm, and that is why her left forearm is placed in a vertical position. John also inclines his head, and the position of his right hand against his cheek is a sign of grief.

The dating of this ensemble of pieces and the identity of the workshop which made them has been the subject of some controversy. The similarity of Mary's headdress with the figure on the frescoes from Taüll has supported the point of view that the pieces were carved in the 12th century, coinciding with the period of Ramon, Bishop of Roda and Barbastro, around 1123 (see the introductory text from section V). Be that as it may, there are certain scholars who argue that some of these works were possibly done in the 13th century.

112 *Figures of the Santa Maria in Taüll Descent from the Cross*

12th OR 13th CENTUR

THE PIECES FROM THIS Descent from the Cross were discovered in 1907 behind the altarpiece of the original church. The figures of Christ, Joseph of Arimathea, the Virgin and a thief —perhaps Dymas— are conserved. Therefore, the figures that should be on the left side of Christ are missing. The set is considered to have come from the Erill Workshop (111), although the carving is simpler than the previous work, which is thought to be a likely model for it. It is interesting to see that Christ has jointed arms, a detail that indicates a later alteration, and his feet are crossed, differing from the one from Erill-la-Vall. In addition, the figure of the thief has his eyes blindfolded, a fact that could have a relation to Cicero's comments on the condemned facing the torture of crucifixion (in the work in which he defends Rabirius to Julius Caesar; *Pro Rabirius*, XVI). The arms are missing from this piece, since it was usual for the arms to be independent of the body. To sum up, everything points to the fact that this ensemble could belong to a later period, to the 13th century.

113 *The Christ from 1147*

CONSECRATED IN THE YEAR 1147
(ACCORDING TO A PARCHMENT FOUND ON THE REAR)

UNLIKE THE FOLLOWING PIECE, this image belongs to the category of the suffering Christ, observed in previous sections (the *Cubells Christ* 1, 6). This is identified as *Christus patiens,* associated by some authors to the Byzantine world. In Western Europe, the oldest example is the one known as the *Gero Christ,* Cologne, which dates from the years 960-80. It can be distinguished by its semi-nudity, covered only by a breech-cloth or *perizonium* (according to the apocryphal text of the Acta of Pontius Pilate), and with the arms slightly bent. At times Christ is depicted with closed eyes, emphasising the idea of His human suffering and His death.

As an exception, this piece can be dated precisely —in the year 1147— when it was consecrated, according to a parchment found in 1952 in a cavity on the back of the figure. A series of relics had been deposited in this hiding-place wrapped in fragments of cloth that are conserved in the Museu Tèxtil i de la Indumentària in Barcelona. Thus, the *Christ from 1147* is a valuable reference point for the dating of similar pieces, and moreover it confirms the function of reliquaries that some of these carvings fulfil. It is also known that it was restored in 1521, which makes it an illustration of the remodelling that has been undertaken in these types of figures through the course of time, as we have already seen in the *Virgin from Ger* (IV, 61) or in the *Frontal from Santa Maria in Taüll* (VII, 107).

As a result of the restoration of 1952, the piece is now exhibited without its polychromy, varnish, or the gold leaf applied in the 16th century, and we can appreciate the careful and highly carving in areas like the abdomen or the facial features. The nose and the pronounced cheekbones should be noted, as well as the beard and peaceful expression on the face. This piece has been linked to a hypothetical workshop of Urgell, but its provenance is unknown, although at times attributed to Andorra.

114 *The Batlló Majesty*

MIDDLE OF THE 12th CENTURY

THE *BATLLÓ MAJESTY* IS without doubt one of the most significant works in the whole collection because it is a capital example of sculptural production in Catalonia in the 12th century. Although its precise origin is unknown, it probably comes from the vicinity of Olot, where the collector Enric Batlló bought it. Subsequently, it has been known by his name.

Among the different varieties of crucifix, this piece is included in the category called 'triumphant', considered to be Oriental in origin, and specifically from Syria. Hence, the figure is superposed on the cross, without showing any sign of suffering due to his sacrifice: his eyes are open, his posture is rigid, his arms are in a horizontal position, and he wears a long-sleeved tunic (*manicata*). This is a clear allusion to the victory of Christ over death. According to most scholars, the prototype of this Western variant is the *Volto Santo* in the Lucca Cathedral (Tuscany). The Lucca Christ —which, as legend has it, arrived in Italy from the Orient in the 8th century— became an increasingly important cult object from at least the 11th century on, and was remade about 1200, following the earlier model. The crucifix in Brunswick Cathedral (Lower Saxony), which is another noteworthy example of this type of work, signed by Imervard in 1173, could also have been inspired by the *Volto Santo*.

One of the notable aspects is the well-preserved polychromy in red and blue. The decoration on the tunic stands out: the design is made up of circles containing floral motifs that recall Oriental textiles. A similarity to a textile from the Cathedral of Roda de Isábena (Huesca) has been claimed. On the other hand, the lower border has certain motifs that might resemble the angular qualities of the Cufic script. In addition, on the upper part of the cross, the following inscription appears: *'IHS NAZARENVS REX IVDEORVM'* (Jesus of Nazareth, King of the Jews), as in other examples. As was customary, there was, on the back, a pictorial representation of the *Agnus Dei*, of which only a few vestiges remain.

According to different scholars, this piece is one of the crowning achievements of the so-called Ripoll Workshop from whence other works of great importance came, such as the *Beget Majesty* (conserved *in situ*). To be sure, there are, among the pieces from this hypothetical workshop, similarities in the postures, attire and the handling of the vertical folds. There are also some examples of more rudimentary work conserved in Catalonia resembling this one. This is the case of the work from the Church of Sant Salvador in Bellver (Museu Episcopal de Vic), or the *Éller Majesty* itself (**IV, 52**). But the *Batlló Majesty* is set apart from the others by the elegant simplicity of its volumes and by the skilful reduction of the facial features to planes and angles. All this, together with its grave and dignified expression, denotes the work of an excellent sculptor.

SECTION IX

Paintings from the Church in Sorpe

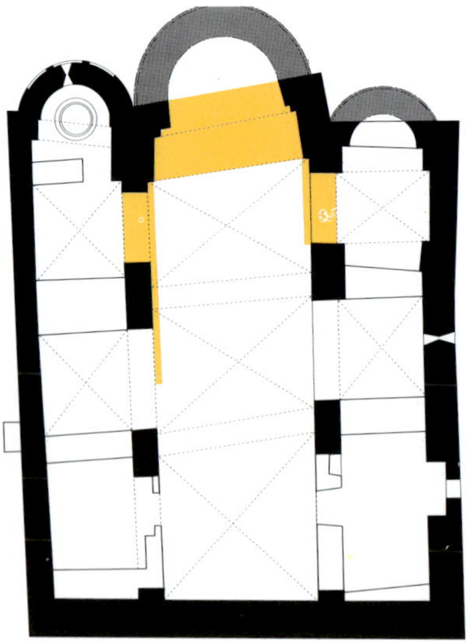

Paintings conserved in the MNAC

THE MUSEUM POSSESSES a remarkable pictorial group from the parish church of Sant Pere in Sorpe which includes the paintings on the two triumphal arches and the ones on a part of the nave. The apse was torn down in the 18th century. The interest of these paintings resides in their iconography —wholly original in certain respects— and because of the question of authorship: it seems that three painters and their respective workshops or assistants worked on the decoration of the church.

The iconographic programme, which is difficult to reconstruct because it is incomplete, reveals an elaborate theological thinking, the meaning of which cannot be exhausted by only one reading. The Old and New Testament are typologically counterposed on the walls of the nave. There are allegorical figures and scenes on the triumphal arches, along with the depiction of several saints. Lastly, sainted martyrs, archangels and signs of the zodiac appear on the intradoses of the arches that lead to the side aisles.

The south wall contained episodes from the Old Testament. The paintings —damaged by humidity— are organised in two band. In the upper band, the scene referring to The Fall can still be identified, and in the lower, the Rivers of Paradise can be seen. Beside the apse on the north wall, the story of the Redemption begins, created by the best of the painters or ateliers that worked in Sorpe. The narration of the story starts with the Annunciation: the angel's announcement to Mary of the birth of Jesus, son of the Almighty. In addition to canonical elements (Luke 1, 26-38), such as the Holy Spirit hovering over the Virgin, there are others that are not mentioned in the Gospels. The first, which was rarely seen in early Byzantine art, is the presence of a half-hidden young woman who regards the scene, as in the paintings from Santa Maria of Castelseprio in Lombardy which date from the 9th century, or in Carolingian ivories from the school of Ada, as that in the Bodleian Library in Oxford. This young woman, watching the angel who announces to Mary that the Lord has

chosen her, is a witness to the mystery of the Incarnation. This woman also appears in the paintings from Saint-Martin-des-Puits, completed around the year 1200 in the French region of Aude. The other apocryphal element in the Annunciation from Sorpe is the Virgin's spindle, frequently seen in Byzantine art but very rarely in Western art. The customary interpretation is that the Virgin was spinning the veil of the Temple. Nevertheless, the image could also

have an allegorical meaning, in the sense that it is in Mary where the two natures of Christ —the human and the divine are spun.

The cycle of Christ's childhood continued towards the west with at least two more scenes: the Visitation —now lost— and the Nativity (Luke 2, 7). This last scene also contains the bath of the Holy Child (*'EMMANVEL'*), mentioned in the

Apocryphal Gospels and often depicted in Byzantine iconography. Below, between the two arches, we can see a splendid representation of the Crucifixion, with Stephanon carrying the sponge and Longinus holding the spear; the grieving Virgin stands nearby. Adam's skull is below the tree of the cross. On the right, over the arch, a thurifer angel appears (*'ANGELVS D[OMI]NI'*). Above the scene, we see the remains of an inscription (*'EHENSVS...ISTA COHORS PLORATO[RVM]'*) doubtlessly referring to the Passion.

The relevant role the Virgin Mary plays in achieving Redemption is emphasised on the first of the two triumphal arches, the one nearest the nave. Both arches are the work of another painter, or in all likelihood of another workshop, different from the painters who worked on the paintings in the nave. To the north we find an image that has become famous: the Virgin with the Holy Child on her lap is seated between two trees, one of them leafy and the other withered: the former symbolizes the Church and the latter, the Synagogue. Mary is the link between the two Laws, between the two Testaments. Over the top of the tree on the right, evoking the seven-branched Jewish candelabrum, the inscription *'S[AN]C[T]A MARIA'* appears, and over the verdant tree on the left, the word *'[R]EX'* referring to Christ.

The scene below is an image of the Church, that of the miraculous haul of fish in the Sea of Tiberias (John 21, 1-9), where the ship representing the Church, with the Chi-Rho or monogram of Christ as its banner, is guided by Andrew, Peter and a third Apostle whose identifying inscription has been lost. Two of them row while the one in the middle pulls in the net full of fish. The ecclesiological and Christological meaning of the image is evident. On the upper part of the arch, on both sides of the keystone, the offerings of Cain and Abel were represented, of which only the vestiges remain.

On the last triumphal arch, the one that was nearest the apse, several saints venerated by the Milan Church are depicted. This is revealing of the origin of the sources, if not of the painters. Above, on both sides of the triumphal arch, the saints Gervasius (*'SCS GERVASIUS'*) and Protasius (*'SCS PROTASIVS'*), stand dressed in rich garments. Below, St. Ambrosius (*'SCS AMBROSIVS'*), the patron saint of the Milan Church and one of the Fathers of the Universal Church, in addition to another saint who is not identified. Below the saints, on both sides of the arch, there are three women's heads without haloes, who could perhaps be identified as the Virtues.

Lastly, the paintings on the intradoses of the arches that separated the nave are clearly the work of another painter or workshop, the least sophisticated of the three involved, which uses a very limited palette of colours. On the intrados of the arch on the north or Gospel side, the saints Felix (*'SCS FELI[CIS]'*) and Pastor (*'PASTO'*) are rendered; they are the first and the last of the martyrs mentioned in a Hispanic liturgical text concerning Daciano's persecution of the Christians. Below the saints are the signs of Gemini (*'GEMINI'*) and Cancer (*'CRANC'*), and a niche, flanked by chalices, that was used to house liturgical objects. The south arch on the Epistle side shows the Holy Spirit on the keystone with two archangels at the sides, and below, an elephant with a tower and the sign for Sagittarius, now extremely deteriorated but remarkable for its pictorial quality. This Sagittarius could be attributed to one of the other painters that worked in the church, possibly the one who did the painting in the nave, providing grounds to think that all the different paintings in the church were done in the same period of time.

The subject of authorship is even more complicated. A mural treating the Crucifixion of Christ (Museu Diocesà d'Urgell) comes from the church of Estaon, near Sorpe, and is so similar to the Sorpe nave that it would have to be attributed to the same painter. In this respect, on the lower part of the crucifixion scene at Sorpe there are remains of an inscription (*'NI ME P'*), the purpose of which has been said to be a signature, ending with the words *'me pinxit'* (I was painted by...). This signature, if it is a signature, would identify the finest painter who worked on the church in Sorpe: the artist who painted the magnificent scene of the Annunciation in the nave, whose style could somehow be compared to that of the Pedret Circle, possibly due to origin and training, and less for reasons of mutual influence. In these Sorpe nave paintings —the ones that show more distinguished pictorial and stylistic qualities— local pigments from the Pyrenees were used, and imported lapis lazuli was used for the blue of Christ *perizonium*, and silver leaf for the suppedaneum of the Cross.

Chronologically, the frescoes from Sorpe must be dated later than the year 1123 since the Virgin that appears on one of the triumphal arches —located between the Church and the Synagogue— must have been done later than the one on the apse from Santa Maria in Taüll, on which it seems to depend stylistically, apart from the narrative quality that can be appreciated in the scenes depicted.

SECTION X

The saints in iconography. The frontal from Durro

THIS SECTION CONSISTS of only one piece, the frontal from the Church of Sant Quirze and Santa Julita in Durro. This piece is the starting point for an inquiry into the iconography of saints and martyrs, which plays an important part in Romanesque art. The lives and martyrdoms of the saints who emulated the example of Jesus Christ became models of behaviour for Christians in their desire to attain eternal life.

Sometimes the representations of saints in Romanesque churches have precise historical connotations and obey political directives which emanated from the Church itself. For example, the depiction of the death of St. Thomas Becket, Archbishop of Canterbury: a death ordered by King Henry II of England in 1170 —and painted on the walls of the Church of Santa Maria in Terrassa soon after the death of the saint. This took place in the atmosphere of the Gregorian reformation, which aspired to a renovation of the clergy and the independence of the Church from royal power. In this sense, the abundant representations of the Seat of St. Peter, —found, for example, on the north apse of Sant Quirze in Pedret (III, 30)— responded to the need to manifest the predominance of Rome and the Holy See over secular power, according to the changes promoted by the Gregorian reform. These are two examples of iconographic subject matter having to do with the saints and their clear relation to the history of the time.

The study of the hagiographic representations can help to identify artistic and cultural trends.

The literary sources for the depiction of the lives of the saints are diverse. In the *Acts of the Apostles*, from the New Testament, the lives of St. Peter, St. John and St. Paul are explained, as well as the life of the protomartyr,

St. Stephen. In the Western Church, the *Martyrology* is the catalogue of martyrs and saints, organised by the day assigned to them. The equivalent in the Eastern Church is the *Menology*, a Byzantine liturgical book containing the lives of the saints, ordered by days and by months so that they can be read on the vigil of their feast day. However, there were also other sources: the narration or *passio* of the martyrdom; the poetic works of Prudentius, Paulinus of Nola, Cassiodorus, Jerome, Augustine, Bede and other authors; the *libelli* or booklets of their miracles; the panegyrics used from the 10th century on, in the procedure leading to canonization; the homilaries, and so forth. In the 13th century, about 1264, a Dominican, the Archbishop of Genova, Iacoppo de Varazze (1230-1290), wrote the *Golden Legend*, a compilation of saints' lives that was widely-read in the Middle Ages. Many translations were made, including one from Roussillon in Catalan.

There are saints who are known throughout the world, like St. Peter and St. Paul, and saints whose worship is strictly local. The depiction of local saints sometimes occurs in places far from their origin, a fact which leads us to suppose that the repertoires and sources that many itinerant artists had available must have helped to spread these images. There is no other way to explain the presence of St. Pierius in Pedret, a saint who was never worshipped in Catalonia.

Something similar could have happened in Sant Pere in Sorpe, where three saints venerated by the Milan Church are depicted: Ambrosius, Bishop of Milan (374), one of the Fathers of the Western Church, and the sainted martyrs Gervasius and Protasius. St. Ambrosius invented the relics of these two saints; he took them to his church, today bearing his name, and he had them deposited below the altar, where he himself would be entombed. The transfer of the relics —carried out with great liturgical pomp, imitating Oriental ceremonies— had great influence in the West, in the history of the worship of the saints and their relics, which was highly important in the Middle Ages. More than for reasons of worship, the inclusion of the three Milanese saints in Sorpe must have conformed to parameters such as those mentioned above —the sources and models used by painters— which in the last instance would refer to their origin.

A different case is that of St. Sernin or Saturninus, the evangelizer of Gaul, martyr and Bishop of Toulouse in Languedoc. The cult of the Toulouse martyr, although known from ancient times in the *Tarraconense*, resurged with new vigour when the Carolingians entered Catalonia in the year 785. The advocation of this saint in Sant Serni de Tavèrnoles is quite significant. It was a very old monastery reformed by the Carolingians to eradicate the adoptionist heresy and to introduce the Roman liturgy and the Benedictine rule. The altar frontal from this monastery (I, 2) is dedicated to this saint.

A parallel case might be that of the bishop and confessor, St. Martin of Tours, who was worshipped throughout Visigothic Hispania, including the *Tarraconense*, at least from the 6th century onwards. A sanctuary and a great basilica were built above his tomb in Tours in order to accomodate the numerous pilgrims who came from far and wide. His sense of charity in sharing his cape with a poor man is depicted on the *Frontal from Ix* (I, 4), where he is on foot —according to Carolingian tradition— and on the *Frontal from Chía* (XIX, 147), where he is on horseback, following the more usual practice. He must have been painted on the walls of Sant Joan in Boí as well, according to the inscription preserved on the north nave (II, 26).

Other saints depicted are the Hispanic martyrs Felix and Pastor (on a side arch in Sorpe, IX, 115), and Eulàlia (on the semicircular area of the apse of Santa Eulàlia in Estaon, XI, 117.)

The work which we use to illustrate the worship of saints is the frontal from Durro, which comes from the chapel of Sant Quirze and Santa Julita in Durro in the Boí Valley. In the central compartment and within a mandorla, as if it were a depiction of the Virgin and Child, the sainted martyrs Julitta and her son Quiricus are seen, identified by inscriptions on the sides. The events connected with their martyrdom are very fanciful and vary depending on the different sources, but according to the *Martyrology of Jerome* they must have been martyrized in Antioch. St. Julitta, in particular, was worshipped widely in Asia Minor and in neighbouring countries, as well as in Gaul and Hispania from ancient times. In Santa Maria Antiqua, in Rome, a cycle of frescoes was dedicated to her in the 8th century. In Durro, the martyrdom of St. Quiricus and St. Julitta —drawn from many sources— is poorly rendered within traditional compositional schemes. The flat colours and the chromatic contrasts are noticeable on this frontal.

SECTION XI

The apse paintings from Estaon and Surp

Apse from Santa Eulàlia in Estaon

THE GREAT PAINTERS who worked in Catalonia between the end of the 11th century and the first half of the 12th must have made a great impact there, and not only among the prominent secular and ecclesiastical dignitaries, the patrons of the imposing churches that had to be decorated. The works of the Pedret Circle, Taüll and the other splendid mural groups that have not survived, but undeniably existed in Catalonia in the Romanesque period, were the models which successive generations of local painters tried to imitate. The impact of the work must have been seen by local artists and painters; some of whom perhaps had been trained in the workshops of those great masters. These local artists, who were painting during the second half of the 12th century, must have found the source of their inspiration in the style of such works. This is evident in many cases, for example, in the paintings on the apse from Estaon and in the church in Surp. The works attributed to the Master of Santa Coloma **(XII, 119 & 120)** and the murals on the apses in Ginestarre and Esterri de Cardós **(IV, 46 & 44)** show this influence in various forms and in differing degrees.

The apse of the old church of Santa Eulàlia in Estaon **(117)** is, stylistically, an ingenuous and technically clumsy derivation of the Pedret Circle style. It is enough to compare the seraphim in Estaon with the ones in Santa Maria d'Àneu **(III, 37)** to verify this statement. Nevertheless, in Estaon, in addition to the artist or the workshop that decorated the apse, other painters more directly influenced by the art produced in Lombardy worked on it too, for example, the painter of the crucifixion conserved in the Museu Diocesà d'Urgell, which is in a very similar style to the one in Sorpe **(IX, 115)**. Moreover, the decoration of the Church of Sant Iscle and Santa Victòria in Surp, from where a depiction of St. John the Evangelist is exhibited **(118)**, is very close in style to one of the painters who worked on the churches in Taüll; the most well-known, the one who is called the Master of the Last Judgement (see the text in Section VII). The Apostle exhibited, together with the other members of the apostolic college, was found on the semicircular part of the church apse. Other fragments of this work are in the Museu Diocesà d'Urgell.

The iconography of the apse from Estaon presents some interesting features. The *Maiestas Domini* rests on a complete circle, recalling the Carolingian age, and is surrounded by the Tetramorph; the anthropozoömorphic eagle of the Evangelist John stands out. The image of Christ is also accompanied by a seraph and a cherub, both of whom are identical. They only differ in the inscriptions assigned to them: *'SCS SERAPHIM'* and *'SCS CHERVBIM'*. Christ is also accompanied by two interceding archangels, Gabriel and Michael wearing phylacteries (*'PETICIVS, POSTVLACIVS'*), which show clearly their character of mediators.

On the semicircular part of the apse, almost in the centre, there is the Baptism of Christ, which the Synoptic Gospels interpret as the solemn inauguration of the ministry of Jesus. The scene acquires the aspect of a Theophany, where the divinity of the Son is revealed by the Father ('This is my beloved Son, in whom I am well pleased', Matthew 3, 13-17; Mark 1, 9-13; Luke 3, 21-22) via the Holy Spirit in the form of a dove. In Estaon, a naked Jesus is in the River Jordan (*'GORDANVS'*) where John baptises Him, the dove of the Holy Spirit overhead. An angel is keeping guard over His clothes. Iconographically, it should be noted that John has an angelical-looking face; he is not dressed as an anchorite, or hermit, but rather in a *manicata* and a *pallium* tunic. His hand is on Jesus's head, with the angel on the other side of the river, as is customary in depictions of this scene.

This scene is flanked by a series of female saints, among whom is the Virgin Mary alongside the Baptism scene. She holds a chalice that has a eucharistic meaning. At her side is St. Eulalia (*'SCS EULALIA'*), whose church this is, and on the other side of the window, there are two other saints: Lucy, and in all likelihood, Agnes. In the right corner, a presbyter saint and an inscription (*'S ECO PBR'*) can be seen. There is a fundamental change regarding the groups we have seen up to now: the substitution of the heavenly court that accompanies the *Maiestas Domini* by a narrative scene concerning the life of Christ, and the depiction of saints whose cult is more limited in scope.

On the lower part of the semicircular apse, superimposed on the simulated drapery as if this were transparent and allowing what is behind to be seen, there are various hunting scenes which sometimes appear in the decoration of other Romanesque churches, in the crypt of the Cathedral of Aquileia (Udine, Italy), for example. In Estaon, a hunter with his net and his dog can be seen, in addition to a great-tusked boar, and another large animal with tusks, among other figures. The subject of the hunt, which comes from Classical Antiquity, has been a part of Christian iconography since ancient times (for example, the mosaics of Centcelles, near Tarragona, in the 4th century), and has a richness of symbolic content which cannot be exhausted by a single reading. In Estaon, this hunting seems to treat the difficulty that exists on the road to perfection; in short, the struggle between good and evil.

Beyond the apse, on both sides of the triumphal arch, a presbyter and a layman face each other; they could be the patrons of the church, as occurs in other instances, such as the Carolingian paintings of San Benedetto de Mals, or Malles, in the Italian Tyrol, and the Romanesque paintings in Saint-Aignan de Brinay, near Bourges.

The Museum has other, albeit more fragmentary, paintings from the Church in Estaon, which are not displayed.

SECTION XII

The paintings from the Santa Coloma Circle in Andorra

THE MASTER OF SANTA COLOMA is the name by which the anonymous painter who decorated the apse of this church in Andorra is known by historiography. Apart from those remaining *in situ*, the main body of the paintings from this church are in Berlin (Staatliche Museen zu Berlin). They are attributed to the same stylistic circle as the paintings on the two apses exhibited in this section: the one from Sant Romà in Les Bons (119) mounted on a flat support, and the one from Sant Miquel in Engolasters (120) on an apsidal support; both of them also come from the valleys of Andorra.

The style of this circle is very easy to recognise, due to faces of the figures with highly specific features which gives them a slightly naïf air. A distant echo of the stylistic influence of the Pedret Circle can be noted, yet reinterpreted in a very particular way. As will be seen, there is also an ingenuousness in the way some iconographic aspects are resolved. For example, the Alpha and Omega hanging one below the other on Christ's left, as if they were ornaments without particular meaning.

The chronology of this stylistic circle has been determined by the date the church of Sant Romà in Les Bons was consecrated by Bishop Bernat Roger of Urgell in 1164, according to a parchment found in the altar. The dating of the paintings of Sant Romà in Les Bons seems to be unquestionable because the altar, which is made of masonry, has the remains of a decoration with ornamental motifs identical to the ones on fragments still existing *in situ*, on the lower part of the apse. However, from the stylistic point of view it can be deduced that the paintings from Sant Romà in Les Bons were not the first ones carried out by this group. The ones from Santa Coloma in the first instance, and secondly those from Engolasters, were probably done before them. Thirdly, we have the paintings from Sant Romà in Les Bons, and lastly the ones from Sant Cristòfol in Anyós, attributed to the same stylistic circle.

Apse from Sant Miquel in Engolasters

The best-preserved work of the group, and the only one exhibited on an apsidal support —a very important question for an understanding of the iconographic programme— is the apse from the small church of Sant Miquel in Engolasters. In the Tetramorph surrounding the *Maiestas Domini* the angel of Matthew has been substituted by Saint Michael, the saint to whom the church is dedicated, represented at the moment of slaying the dragon. As for the rest of the symbols, both the symbol for Mark and the one for Luke are found within the tiny medallions carried by angels. The eagle of John is remarkable for its beauty.

SECTION XIII

Art around 1200

SEVERAL PICTORIAL WORKS that variously reflect the great renewal experienced in Western art arount 1200 have been brought together in this section. The dates of this renewal are approximately 1180 —the year in which the goldsmith Nicholas of Verdun was already active— to 1230, although this date is sometimes advanced a few more years. This renewal, which also influenced the arts of the miniature, sculpture and metalwork, was motivated in large part by the influence of Byzantine art in the era of the dynasty of the Comnenes (1081-1185), characterised by the emphasis placed on the volumes of the human body and by the treatment of facial features, which were very elaborately modelled. However, other factors contributed to shape the art of 1200, as for example, the incorporation of new iconographic subjects, some of them belonging to Western art. A paradigmatic example of the multiplicity of influences in the art of 1200 is the altar from Lluçà (Museu Episcopal de Vic), where one of the characteristic subjects of Western art is depicted: the Coronation of the Virgin, which could be a creation of Abbot Suger of Saint-Denis. Another formulation, albeit little-developed, of this subject would be the Gothic portal from Senlis in northern France, from *c.* 1170. This scene in a Byzantine style is depicted with great intensity on the altar from Lluçà.

The strong influence of Byzantine art on the Western arts, which greatly conditions what we understand as the style of 1200, can be deduced from the output of different artistic centres. Among these, the island of Sicily was one of the most important, being where King Roger II (1095-1154) and his son King William I (1120-66) invited Greek mosaicists to decorate the churches of Cefalú, Palermo and Monreale with extended iconographic cycles. It appears that in all probability English artists were working in some of these places: they had probably gone there with the entourage of Joan, daughter of Henry II of England, who married King William of Sicily in 1177. Afterward these artists must have done part of the illumination of the *Winchester Bible,* and then later painted the murals of Sigena (XXI, 152), a nunnery founded by Queen Sancha, the wife of Alfons I of Catalonia and II of Aragon.

But Sicily was not the only route of Byzantine penetration into the West. Greek mosaicists also worked in Torcello, Murano and San Marcos in Venice, places from which the Byzantine influence must have also spread. Moreover, princes, magnates and ecclesiastic dignitaries brought back Byzantine reliquaries, icons and manuscripts from their pilgrimages to the Holy Land, objects which were much admired in the West. Other objects of this type arrived through trade routes or as gifts and presents from royal ambassadors or delegations, such as the staurotheke from the Cathedral of Esztergom in Hungary, which could have been presented by an emperor from the dynasty of the Comnenes before 1190. We must also take into account the emigration of Greek and Byzantine artists to the West and the subsequent importation of Byzantine work and treasures during the Latin Empire of Constantinople (1204-61).

Of the works exhibited in this section those that reveal the greatest Byzantine influence are the murals from Andorra la Vella **121**, and especially the *Frontal from Baltarga* **123**, which can be attributed to a painter who, if not Greek or Byzantine in origin, at least possessed a very Hellenistic outlook. This painter can be linked to Master Alexander, who signed the missing *Frontal from Saint-Genis-des-Fontaines* (Roussillon). This frontal and the *Frontal from Orellà* (Oreilla, Conflent) are the nearest parallels to the *Frontal from Baltarga.* The most noticeable features in this work are the quasi-sculptural and compact quality of the bodies of the figures and the modelling of the faces, all following the example of Byzantine models.

The Byzantine tendency represented by the *Frontal from Baltarga* did not, however, have much influence in Catalonia. The opposite thing occurred in the case of the style of the *Frontal from Avià* **122**, where the Byzantine influence, although easily detectable in, for example, the faces, is generally more attenuated. The *Frontal from Avià* and the *Frontal from Rotgers* (Museu Episcopal de Vic) would be the most important works from an important atelier, one which exercised great influence in the Catalan painting of the age; this will be explained further in the commentary on the piece **122**.

This Byzantine style is also seen in the paintings from Andorra la Vella, where it can be observed, for instance, in the features and modelling of the face in *The*

Mocking of Christ, using shading and highlights, and in the figures on the north apsidiole. Furthermore some of their iconographic subjects are typically Byzantine. This is especially obvious in the scene of the Washing of the Feet, which is conserved in a private collection. The Byzantine influence in Andorra has been related to Germanic and Austrian workshops in Central Europe belonging to the Salzburg School. The decoration of the chapel of Castel Appiano has also been linked to these, as well as other murals from the Alto Adige (Italy).

From the Byzantine influences of about 1200 emerged in England and the north of France what is commonly called the Channel Style, the repercussions of which are to be observed in one of the pieces exhibited in this section, the so-called *Beam of the Passion* **125**, which is closely linked to a part of the illumination of the *Liber Feudorum Maior* in the Arxiu de la Corona d'Aragó in Barcelona, for the type of figures and the way of grouping them, as well as for the polychromy. It has also been connected to the *Beatus of Las Huelgas,* dated 1220 (Pierpont Morgan Library, New York).

On the other hand the *Cardet Beam* (126), linked to the later works of the Ribagorça Workshop (XIX), especially to the frontal that comes from the same church in Cardet (IV, 66), has been placed in this section for reasons of typology. Many of these beams were located in the entrance to the apse, as in the case of Toses (XVI, 141), and had joins for fastening images over the altar and in some cases for suspending a Eucharistic dove (XV, 133) or a cross. On the front side of the *Cardet Beam,* there is a succession of scenes showing pairs of birds and other animals facing each other. Peacocks drinking from a chalice can be seen, as well as the struggle of men against monsters. The symbolic meaning that can be inferred is the struggle between good and evil, except in the case of the peacocks which are a symbol of the Christian drinking from the chalice of Salvation. The group, however, has a strong ornamental quality.

The *Tavèrnoles Baldachin* (124), which has been hung at an angle to suggest the original placement of the object over the altar, enables us to observe how the partly destroyed faces of the angels exemplify the art of 1200. On the other hand, the movement shown in the rendering of the bodies is very similar to the angels of Orós (143) and would relate more to Gothic models. An example of this would be the figure of Christ who carries an open book with the inscription: *'EGO SUM VIA, VERITAS ET VITA',* 'I am the way, the truth and the life'.

121 *Paintings from Sant Esteve in Andorra la Vella*

C. 1200-10

THE PAINTINGS FROM the parish church of Sant Esteve in Andorra la Vella are interesting because of their style — where the Byzantine influences of 1200 can be observed— and because of the iconography.

The Museum possesses the paintings from the north apsidiole and various fragments that come from the decoration of the main apse, such as the ox of Luke, the decorative band of fleshy leaves that separates the vaulting of the semicircular part of the apse, and two more fragments that form part of the last of the four scenes of the Passion that used to exist on the semicircular part of the apse. The first one on the left, the Washing of the Feet, was followed by the Seizing and the Flagellation of Christ, all three in private collections. The last one was a combined image of the Mocking and the crown of thorns (Matthew 27, 27-30; Mark 15, 16-19; John 19, 2-3) with Jesus before the Sanhedrin.

On the vaulting of the apsidiole there are two scenes in juxtaposition. The one on the right depicts the angel that announces the birth of John the Baptist to Zachariah (Luke 1, 8-21), with the people who witness the marvel

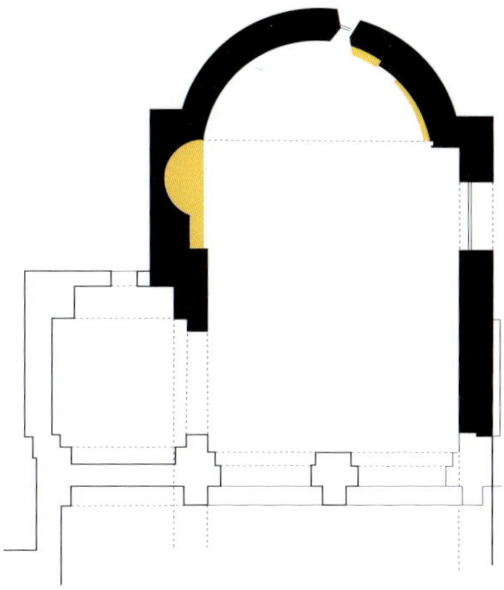

Paintings conserved in the MNAC

standing behind the priest. The one on the left is John the Baptist as an anchorite. Outside the arch there is an acrobatic-looking individual who is filling three jars at a time. These three jars symbolise the Trinity, and the person filling the jars can be identified as one of the servants at the weddings of Canaan, because the same image of this biblical scene is found in Ottonian manuscripts. Furthermore, the sacramental symbol of water, implicit in these scenes, an announcement of renewal and sacrifice, would probably indicate that this small apse contained baptismal fonts.

122 *Altar frontal from Avià*

C. 1170-90

THE FRONTAL THAT comes from the Chapel of Santa Maria in Avià is one of the most outstanding panel paintings of this period in Catalonia. Its style shows the Byzantine influence of the time, an influence that arrived here via English paintings and miniatures (*Psalter of Eadwine,* in Trinity College, Cambridge). In Avià, the drawing of the faces and the modelling of the bodies by means of the folds of drapery and the play of light and shadows, show the liveliness of this Byzantine influence. Nevertheless, in this case the influence is slighter and more pleasing than in other works, for example the *Frontal from Baltarga* (123). Stylistically, the piece closest to the *Frontal from Avià* is the one from Sant Sadurní de Rotgers, in the Museu Episcopal de Vic. The *Frontal from Ribesaltes* (Stiftung Abegg, Riggisberg, Switzerland), the *Frontal from Sant Llorenç*

—partially conserved in the MNAC reserve collection— and the so-called *Baldachin from Toses* (V, 81) are also connected to these. More popular versions within the same tendency are the *Altar from Angostrina* (Angoustrine, Cerdagne) and the *Frontal from Vidrà* (Museu Episcopal de Vic). In the *Frontal from Avià,* the configuring of the angel, its sculptural treatment and the movement of the bodies in the representation of the Magi in the Epiphany are all noteworthy. In the centre of the images, the Holy Child —whose face is very Byzantine— seems not to be blessing the Three Kings, but instead the first scenes of the story of the Redemption, the Annunciation and the Visitation, which are in the upper left corner. The scene of the Birth of Jesus which follows Byzantine examples is very interesting, as is the Presentation of Jesus in the Temple located on the lower right. Here, the priest Simeon appears with covered hands as a sign of respect, giving Jesus to his Mother, Mary, who stretches out her covered arms to receive him. The Holy Child is on the altar, a heralding of his redeeming sacrifice.

123 *Altar frontal from Baltarga*

C. 1200

THE *FRONTAL FROM* *Baltarga* is probably the work in this section in which the art of the year 1200 is shown to be most thoroughly Byzantine: so much so that it could be argued that it is attributable to a Greek painter, or at least to someone strongly influenced by Hellenistic art. This is quite evident in the treatment of the faces, in particular the face of Christ; they are only comparable to the faces on the *Frontal*

from Orellà (Oreilla, Conflent) *in situ*, which R. Ch. Post believed was done by the same hand, or to other Byzantine works. It is very interesting that M. Durliat linked the *Frontal from Orellà* with the unfortunately destroyed *Frontal from Saint-Genis-des-Fontaines*, Roussillon, signed by *'Magister Alexander'*.

Both the *Frontal from Baltarga* and the *Frontal of Orellà* are known for the emphatic volumes of a sculptural quality and the chromatic contrasts between the yellow and the red, set off by the black.

Iconographically, the representation of the martyrdom of St. Andrew —whose name is that of the parish church— in front of the proconsul Aegeas should be noted. On the other hand, the cross does not have the shape that would be more usual in the West. However, the typology of the cross is not a determining factor in the origins of the iconography, because both forms belong to two ancient traditions which are Byzantine in origin.

The date of the frontal must be later than 1198, the year the church was plundered by the troops of the Viscount of Castellbò and the Count of Foix at the height of the Albigensian rebellion.

125 *Beam of the Passion*

C. 1200-20

NO ONE KNOWS where the original beam comes from, nor is it known if it formed part of a baldachin similar to the beams that held the panel of the *Baldachin from Tost* in place (III, 47), conserved in the Museu Episcopal de Vic, and the panel of the *Tavèrnoles Baldachin* (124). It also could have been a cross-beam, like the one on the apse of Toses (XVI, 141) that was used to fasten images in place or to suspend a cross or Eucharistic dove (XV, 133).

It contains seven episodes of the Passion of Christ, one beside the other. From left to right there are: the Seizing of Christ —and Judas' words of greeting, *'AVE RABI'*; the Flagellation; the Road to Calvary *'IHS'*; the Crucifixion —partially lost when the beam was re-utilised later— that includes the words *'QUID AD NOS'*, pronounced by the Jews; the Descent from the Cross (*'NICODEMVS, IOSEP DE ARIM ...'*); and the next scene, the Lamentation over the dead Christ, which is Byzantine in origin (*Epitaphios Threnos).* In this scene, Joseph of Arimathea and Nicodemus are depicted; they deposit the body of Jesus, while the Virgin, St. John and Mary Magdalene weep for Him. The last scene is the Resurrection which used to include the three Marys in the Sepulchre; a seated angel can still be discerned. Jesus is beardless in the Hellenist manner in all the episodes; the various executioners have dark faces as if they were from Ethiopia, according to an ancient Byzantine tradition.

The extremely meticulous and detailed facture of the paintings would indicate that this is the work of a miniaturist whose art is closely related to the second and best illustrator of the *Liber Feudorum Maior*, a royal chartulary (Arxiu de la Corona d'Aragó in Barcelona) which must date from 1172 to 1196. As has been mentioned before, stylistically the beam has also been related, albeit more indirectly, to the 1220 *Beatus of Las Huelgas* (Pierpont Morgan Library, New York), which originally came from this Cistercian monastery in Burgos.

SECTION XIV

The atrium paintings from Sant Vicenç in Cardona

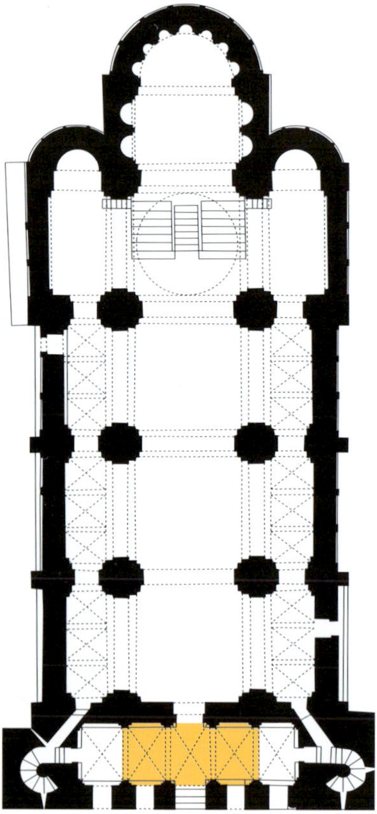

Paintings conserved in the MNAC

THE CARDONA ATRIUM is at the main entrance to the magnificent Church of Sant Vicenç situated in Cardona Castle, built, as the documents show, between 1029 and 1040. It was consecrated with much solemnity in the latter year by the Bishop of Urgell, who was accompanied by the Bishop of Roda de Ribagorça. It is the most monumental and paradigmatic of the churches showing the influence of Lombardy preserved in Catalonia. This church was the seat of a canonical community, which was remodelled in the middle of the 12th century to conform to the Augustinian rule.

The paintings conserved from the atrium of Cardona, which form part of the permanent exhibition for the first time, are those from three central sections of the five in the atrium. Beginning with those paintings, one can deduce that they must have formed part of a larger iconographic programme which extended throughout the atrium. However, for reasons unknown, it

appears that this programme was not completed, and that the two sections at the ends of the atrium were never painted.

These atrium paintings do not correspond to the moment of the construction of the Lombardy-style building, but are somewhat later. They were painted well into the second half of the 12th century, except for one of the scenes, that of the Defence of Girona on the flat wall to the left which, as will be explained below, is much later. The fact that this representation was included later would tend to imply that the decorative programme remained incomplete.

In all, there are five different painted spaces: the groin vaulting of three central sections, and the two flat walls on either side of the central doorway, where the entrance to the church was. On the central vault we see the *Maiestas Domini* surrounded by the Tetramorph. On the left-side vault, the Presentation of Jesus in the Temple is depicted, and on the one on the right, of which only the lower half is preserved, the Assumption of the Virgin, in a double mandorla carried by angels. On the lower wall, the Flagellation can be seen. Lastly, the one on the flat wall on the left is the historic episode of the Defence of Girona.

As for the iconography of the preserved paintings, the scene of the Presentation (Luke 2, 35-8), which also appears on the *Frontal from Avià* **(XIII, 122)**, is centred on

the Infant Jesus situated above the altar; Mary presents Him to the priest Simeon, with the prophetess Anna behind him. The person behind the Virgin is St. Joseph; he carries the propitiatory offering of the young doves. Outside the temple and the circle that encloses the scene, and on the medallions above and below, one can see angels from the waist up; while on the four angles around this there were prophets wearing long phylacteries. The inscriptions that should be on the latter have not been preserved.

As for the Flagellation, the composition is built around the central column to which Jesus is tied, against a background of transversal blue bands bordered in red which, like the other scenes mentioned above, also contain inscriptions. On the extreme right, one of the executioners appears with his scourge raised, and on the other side two other individuals, one of whom holds a long sword.

For reasons of style, these paintings have been related to the ones from Sant Salvador in Polinyà (Museu Diocesà de Barcelona), to others from Santa Maria in Barberà (*in situ*), and to those from Sant Martí Sescorts (Museu Episcopal de Vic), all of them linked to trends of French origin. It must be said, to begin with, that the stylistic affinities between the Cardona atrium and the two first groups mentioned above are much closer. As for the third, most similarity is found in the background motif against which the symbols of the Evangelists are disposed.

On the other hand, despite the apparent modernity of the scene of the Flagellation, the style of the figures, faces and hands, plus the structure of the bodies, is the same in the whole group of paintings described up to now. The scenes or images are also framed in the same way: dark blue bands, bordered with red, in which the inscriptions, now lost or illegible, once were. The horizontal bands which, in traversing the column of the Flagellation form a kind of cross, are handled in the same way. Only one of the walls, the one on the left below the Presentation, which was left unpainted at the beginning, is posterior to the other paintings. On it there is represented, using an already Gothic language, the heroic gesture of Viscount Ramon Folc VI of Cardona, who leads his troops in the defence of the city of Girona against the enemy, the army of the French king Philip the Bold, who had laid siege to the town in 1285. It is very probable that the Viscount of Cardona, who must have commissioned the fresco, would prefer to be remembered for the heroic aspect of his loyalty to the king rather than for his earlier uprising against him.

SECTION XV

Metalwork and enamelling

THE THREE SHOWCASES in this section contain a selection of metal objects (copper, bronze) very often decorated with applications of enamel. Some objects of this type have been seen before in relation to iconography (IV) and church furniture (V), with certain aspects, like typologies, functions and subject matter, having been already touched upon. In this section, the pieces are shown as examples of the activity of a certain type of workshop, and as a reflection of the importance of the sumptuary arts in the Romanesque period. The former is inscribed within another of the major areas of study in relation to Romanesque art, the applied arts (at times subsumed under the obsolete term of the *minor arts*).

The application and richness of these techniques extends beyond the objects conserved in the Museum. Thus, the documented accounts and descriptions of the period bear witness to the existence of sumptuous artefacts made in gold or silver and encrusted with precious gems. Examples of this are the altar frontals of some Catalan cathedrals and monasteries in the 11th and 12th centuries, such as those which existed in Santa Maria in Ripoll which, according to an inventory made in the 12th century, were six in number, one of these being commissioned by Abbot Oliba and made in gold. We should also mention the four altar frontals in Girona Cathedral (one of gold, and three of silver), which are referred to in a 13th-century inventory and among which we might note the one which relied on a donation (of 300 ounces of gold) from the Countess Ermessenda in 1038. With certain exceptions, such economically valuable pieces have disappeared, due to theft or because they have been melted down for their gold or silver.

Rising demand encouraged the development of techniques and more practical procedures, with recourse to cheaper and more easily available materials. Therefore, most of the pieces that have been preserved are made of enamelled copper using the *champlevé* technique. This procedure consists of making cavities in the metal sheet and later filling them with enamel obtained from the fusion of powdered glass. Originating in workshops such as the one in Conques, *champlevé* displaced *cloisonné* in Western Europe. The *cloisonné* technique, typical of the Byzantine world, and frequent in the centuries preceding the Romanesque period, consisted of the application of colour in alveolae, smalls cells delimited by thin metallic strips of gold or copper soldered at right angles to the surface to be decorated.

At this time in Western Europe, some of the most important centres were located in the regions of the Rhine and the Meuse, in Saxony, in the south of France and in Castile, in workshops like the ones in Liège, Cologne, Limoges and Silos, among others. There also must have been more local workshops which emulated the procedures and models of the more important ones. It should be remembered that on the whole, all these workshops made their pieces using the *champlevé* technique. The most obvious characteristic of many of the pieces conserved in Catalonia —and of many of those exhibited in the Romanesque Gallery— is their Limousin origin. Nevertheless, there are important exceptions such as: the cross from the Museu Diocesà d'Urgell, which comes from Palau de Noguera, has been linked to the Silos workshop, to which some candlesticks like the ones on display have been attributed (V, 74); the *Saint Ruf missal bindings,* from the Tortosa Cathedral, which could be the work of a Provençal workshop; and lastly, the spherical *Censer* in the Museum (V, 73), displayed in an earlier section, almost unanimously attributed to a local workshop in Catalonia.

The great number of Limoges objects exhibited demonstrates, when taken together, the success of this centre of production, the works of which are equally encountered in other parts of Europe. Its expansion begins in the third quarter of the 12th century —1167-69 to be precise— when documentary evidence is found of the denomination *opus lemovicense* (work from Limoges). However, in the course of the 13th century, rising demand brought about a tendency to repeat the stereotypes and to turn out pieces of mediocre quality.

On the whole, works from Limoges are much more than a simple version of works made in gold and silver. Account must be taken of the fact that enamelling, together with the gilding which covered the copper base also satisfied the desire for ostentation of the time and also reflected the medieval taste for things that shone. The visual impact resulting from the combination of coloured areas of enamelled and gilded copper, be it flat or in relief, should be appreciated. In addition, the use of these materials favoured the interpretation of the motifs that decorated the objects, and their conservation, unlike gold or silver pieces which were embossed.

Nevertheless, within this range of objects, there are also works commissioned by the nobility, the ecclesiastic authorities or by the Papacy itself. Furthermore, different synodal decisions could have contributed to the spreading of certain types of objects. For example, as a result of the Council of Lateran in 1215, at the time of Pope Innocent III, it was decided that all churches had to possess two pyxes, one of which could be from Limoges (153).

Not all the objects from the precious metalworking ateliers were necessarily enamelled. There were copper pieces that were simply finished with gilt and engraving. Although this kind of work was also done in Limoges, it is very likely that some of these pieces were done in local workshops. Probably this is the case of some of the censers that are on display. The decorative designs used on these were usually of either a plant (128) or architectural nature (129). Architectural decoration will be treated later in relation to an enamelled piece **131**. On the other hand, we have already seen in other sections (1, 8, for example) figures of the Crucified made in bronze, in engraved and gilded relief, which were mounted on a cross (136).

The diversity of technical resources employed in Limoges products is perfectly visible in the three pieces exhibited in the showcase in the middle of this section. The *Mondoñedo crozier* **134** shows the use of engraved figures in relief (on the dragons round the knob); the application of small pieces like the wings of the Archangel Michael; and the use of glass paste to accentuate the eyes of some of the figures. This material also appears in the cabochons that imitate precious stones, as can be seen in the *Incense boat from Ars* (132). Another essential component is obviously the colour. The difference in the colour palette depends on the workshops where they were made, and the material used for their preparation. In Limoges, one of the colours most employed is blue, which appears in several tones. The *Reliquary casket* dedicated to the Slaughter of the Innocents (137) is an example of this: lapis lazuli for the background; turquoise for the throne of King Herod (depicted on the left); and other gradated hues, such as lavender blue, the lightest colour in the floral motif that can be seen in the upper left-hand corner of the scene. The preponderance of blue can sometimes be explained by the fact that this colour may symbolise the Kingdom of Heaven. Red, yellow, white and the different hues of green can also be observed in the motifs on this casket; this is common in many other enamelled objects linked to Limoges. The application of several colours in the same compartment is frequent; for example on the *Eucharistic Dove* **133** in the area around the wings, which is common in this type of piece.

As it is difficult to date these pieces with precision either by their style or by the technical resources employed, the works selected reflect some of the solutions that were most frequently adopted in objects proceeding from Limoges. Different procedures were arrived then, based on the combination of enamelled and copper surfaces. Firstly, enamelled figures with a gilt background are seen on the *Ciborium from La Cerdanya* **135**; and secondly, the combination of flat engraved figures reserved on an enamel background. On some of these, the heads of the figures are often applied in relief, as on the *Châsse* where the *Maiestas Domini* is depicted surrounded by the Tetramorph and angels on the lid, in addition to the Crucifixion on the main face of the piece (139). However, it should be understood that more stereotyped formulas are used on some of the examples: the crude treatment of applied figures which all have the same shape as on objects such as the *Châsse* (138) and the *Christ on the Cross* (140) exhibited in the showcase. The limited range of colours on these pieces and the poor handling of the figures can also be observed: the figures are often reduced to geometricising and irregular forms, as on the aforementioned châsse.

131 *Censer*

SECOND HALF OF THE 13TH CENTURY

THIS CENSER IS distinguished by the decoration on the domed lid, comprised of arches and figures of enamelled angels. Because of these motifs, it is close to the type of censers that symbolised celestial Jerusalem during the 12th century; for example, the *Gozbert censer*, that was commissioned *c.* 1100 and made in the workshops of Treves. The celestial Jerusalem theme evokes the Church in all its perfection, Paradise.

The shape and decoration on different censers which have been dated to the 13th century are a reminder of those mentioned above. These are more simplified works the deeper meaning of which is either diminished or altogether lost. This must apply to the piece here. The same can be said of the other censer displayed in the same showcase (130); it still has the chains that were used to hang and swing it by.

133 *Eucharistic Dove*

FIRST HALF OF THE 13TH CENTURY

HERE WE HAVE a vessel in the form of a dove, used as a receptacle for consecrated wafers. The use of these objects has been known since early Christian times, from the 3rd century onwards. Some Eucharistic Doves were wrought in precious metals, but they have disappeared and are only known through written evidence of their existence. These objects are also one of the typical products from Limoges since the beginning of the 13th century.

The body of the dove is comprised of several conjoined sheets of copper, and the decoration is engraved and enamelled. It is interesting to observe the placement of three or four different colours in each of the concave lines on the wings, which is common in some of these examples. On the base of the piece —where some enamelling is missing— there are holes for the chains that were used to suspend it. It should be remembered that the Eucharistic Doves were hung to evoke the presence of the Holy Spirit during the Eucharist.

134 *Mondoñedo crozier*

C. 1200

THE FIRST ACCOUNT of the existence of this crozier appeared in 1746, when, it is said, it was found in the old Cathedral of Ribadeo, Galicia; it is attributed to Bishop Pelayo of Cebeyra. Later, in the 19th century, the object was moved to the Cathedral of Mondoñedo —also in Galicia— and is the place from which it takes its name. Apart from being one of the few exhibited enamelled works for which a document provenance exists, it is interesting for its decoration. St. Michael killing the dragon on the volute, a subject we have seen earlier (III, 34), is habitual in this type of piece. It displays the head of the dragon turned to face the Archangel's spear, which penetrates its body: this is one of the many depictions of this scene found in the output of Limoges. The dating of the crozier has been generally accepted as being from between 1199 and 1218, the period of the prelature of Bishop Pelayo.

135 *Ciborium from Cerdanya*

C. 1195-1200

THE CIBORIUM FROM Cerdanya, which comes from an undetermined church of this region, consists of the cup and its lid which are formed by two half-spherical metal pieces. The foot is missing and so a part of the crown; one of the other ciboriums exhibited **(IV, 76)** still has its foot. The decoration, arranged as a system of diamonds and triangles with curved sides, is the most notable aspect of the piece. It shows a number of figures from the waist up on a gilt background and inscribed in the aforementioned space, albeit linked in pairs and accompanied by different inscriptions. On the lid we find the angel's greeting to Mary (*'AVE MARIA GRATIA PLENA DOMINUS TECUM'*), and the first twelve letters of the Latin alphabet. The inscription on the cup, however, has never been interpreted. On the inner surfaces of the object, there is also a figuration similar to that which decorates the inside of the *Ciborium from Alpais* (Musée du Louvre). The *Ciborium from Cerdanya* has been linked to a workshop in Limoges, the one known as that of the 'wide eyes'. It is one of the oldest examples of wares from Limoges in Catalonia, dating from the end of the 12th century.

SECTION XVI

The paintings from the apse of Toses

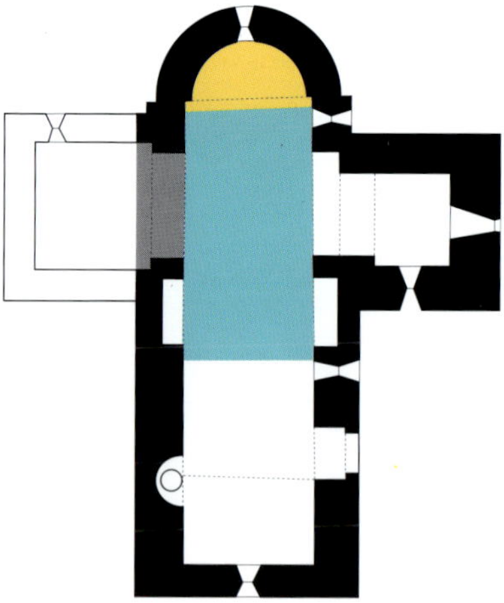

Paintings conserved in the MNAC
Paintings conserved *in situ*

THE APSE OF SANT Cristòfol in Toses is a work from well into 13th century which still calls on Romanesque iconography, although the discreet style already uses a language closer to the Gothic. The new element, here, is the cross-beam, which is absolutely contemporary with the murals. Rather than structural, its function is decorative or, perhaps, practical: for supporting some kind of image. Although there is no proof, it is quite likely that the *Cardet Beam* (XIII, 126) may also have been used for this. The decorated border of the *Toses Beam* is, on the other hand, also very characteristic of the intrados of some Gothic arcades from the end of the 13th century; this also helps to establish a chronologically advanced date for the decoration as a whole. Such a date would be confirmed by the paintings on the vaulting of the church nave still preserved *in situ*, where some fragments of a Last Supper can be seen.

If, as we have already mentioned, the style of the mural group is of a late date, and close in that sense and in some aspects to works like the paintings in El Bruc (*in situ*), Santa Maria in Terrassa —now transferred to canvas and conserved in the church—, and Mosoll (in the MNAC reserve collection), the iconography on the apse of Toses is, however, totally Romanesque. Christ in Majesty on the vaulting is seated on a cushioned throne; the lion symbolising Mark, and the ox for Luke are at either side. There is almost no room for the other two symbols, which are not preserved. The border that separates the vaulting has quite an elaborate plant design. There are only a few vestiges of the Apostles that used to be on the semicircular wall. The offerings of Cain and Abel are depicted on the intrados of the apse window; the lamb offered by Abel is continued outside the window area. Its eucharistic character is revealed in the prayer said at Mass: 'Lord, accept this offering, as You accepted the gifts of the righteous Abel'.

SECTION XVII

Angels in iconography. The frontal of the Archangels

THE WORD *ANGEL* comes from a Greek term meaning messenger or herald. The supernatural existence of angels, and their role as God's messengers or intermediaries between God and man, is an essential element of the mystery of the Christian faith and a dogma of Catholic Church since the Council of Lateran in 1215. In the 5th century, Pseudo-Dionysius, the Areopagite, developed a hierarchy of nine angelical choirs —later reivindicated by scholasticism— that in turn is divided into three categories. The highest includes the Seraphim, the Cherubim and the Thrones; afterward comes the category of the Dominations, the Virtues, the Powers; and lastly, the Principalities, the Archangels, and the Guardian Angels, who are nearest to man. The first and third categories of angels are those that are preeminent in Romanesque iconography, which takes them to be the heavenly court surrounding the Lord in a context of Theophany normally developed in the paintings on apsidal vaulting (see IV, 44; XI, 117). There are also archangels dressed as dignitaries of a Byzantine court who present advocatory inscriptions defending the cause of the Righteous before God.

The archangels Michael, Gabriel and Raphael, present, for example, on the apse of Santa Maria d'Àneu, where seraphim (III, 37) are also depicted, also appear on other occasions. Michael, as prince of the angels and defender of God's people, defeats the dragon, exactly as depicted in one of the compartments of this *Frontal of the Archangels* (142), titled thus because the archangels are its protagonists. The struggle between Michael and the dragon is explicit in the inscription: '*MICHAEL P(RE)LIABATVR CV(M)DRACONE*'. Other versions of his struggle against the dragon can be admired in the Romanesque art collection, as on the apse from *Sant Miquel in Engolasters* (XII, 120) and on the *Mondoñedo crozier* (XV, 134). Michael is also recognised as having the function of a *psychopomp*, or one who leads souls to God. Moreover, when Judgment Day comes at the end of time and so as to separate the good from the bad, Michael will weigh up the action of each individual soul, an act known as *psychostasis*, as depicted here, and also on the west wall of Santa Maria in Taüll (VII, 102). The pronounced narrative and anecdotal sense of the frontal is evident in the inclusion of a devil who tries trick Michael and unbalance the scales in his favour. This subject was already present in ancient Oriental art.

The miracle of Monte Gargano is represented in the neighbouring compartment. On the mountain chosen by Michael to build his sanctuary, the ox which is his symbol is seen. A hunter attempts to harm the latter, but miraculously the hunter's arrow turns and strikes him in the eye. The inscription, '*I(n)VE(n)CIO S(ANCT)I MICHAELIS*', refers to this episode related to St. Michael. This legendary deed of the hunter and the ox would later be quite frequent in Gothic painting, in the same way that Gothic funerary sculpture would repeat the scene of the archangels Raphael and Gabriel transporting a soul to heaven, as can be seen in the upper left compartment. Gabriel plays a very important role as God's messenger in the Annunciation. It is not depicted here, but can be seen on the frontals from Cardet, Mosoll (IV, 66 y 67), Avià (XIII, 122) and Rigatell (XIX, 148), and on the frescoes from Sant Pere in Sorpe (IX, 115).

The Frontal of the Archangels is, stylistically speaking, a work close to the Gothic, painted with great delicacy and elaborate graphic touches which has been linked to the author of the murals from Sant Pau in Casserres (Museu Diocesà i Comarcal de Solsona), and also to the altar and the Christ from Lluçà (Museu Episcopal de Vic). In contrast to the apse of Toses (XVI, 141) located beside it, *the Frontal of the Archangels* is an innovatory work and yet is close to the legacy of the 1200 style. Above all, it is a piece of great artistic quality.

SECTION XVIII

Other works from the 13th century

THE HISTORICAL PERIOD that takes us to the coinage minted by Kings Alfons I the Chaste and James I the Conqueror exhibited here, represents the beginning of the expansion of the Catalan-Aragonese Crown throughout the Mediterranean. Although the paintings in this section belong to that period, they are not innovatory works, but rather follow the traditions of the years prior to the great artistic upsurge of the end of the 13th century, which can be seen in the galleries devoted to Gothic art.

As for the paintings displayed, the dominant note is the survival of formal schemes and iconography within a diversity of styles. On the two panels of the *Altar from Orós* (143), the angels carrying the mandorla in which St. Peter is portrayed are depicted according to the preestablished norms, while the angels alongside St. Paul show more movement. The similarity of these two side panels to the *Baldachin from Tost* (IV, 47), and in a lesser degree to the *Tavèrnoles Baldachin* (XIII, 124), is quite obvious. The style of the side panels of Orós recalls the artistic technique of stained-glass windows because of the use of flat colours and of figures delimited by thick black lines, as if of lead.

In the *Frontal from Farrera* (144) —more naive in character and draughtmanship— one can observe a distant echo of the tradition of 1200. The movement of the figures and their facial features demonstrates this popular and late derivation from more elaborate models of the 1200 style; the same is true of the depiction of the lion symbolising Mark. The compositional scheme of the frontal is one that has been seen earlier, with the figure of Christ in Majesty in the central compartment surrounded by the Tetramorph, with the Apostles at the sides arranged in superposed bands of three figures. The *Frontal from Farrera* has a certain kinship to the frontal of the *Altar from Sant Romà de Vila* (V, 82), although in the latter the number of Apostles is fewer. The effigy of St. Catherine (145), from Isavarre, much more rudimentary and rustic in style, is a late example of ancient models. This portrait of the saint was placed over one of the windows on the semicircular part of the apse. Other fragments of decoration from the apse,

Altar side panels from Orós

such as different Apostles, crowned figures within medallions and an animal-musician are disseminated between the Art Museum of Toledo, Ohio, the Kunstmuseum in Basel and the Museu Diocesà d'Urgell.

146 *Royal coinage*

146.4

FOLLOWING THE UNION, in 1137, of the Catalan and Aragonese crowns, a period of expansion begins, first into Occitania and then Majorca and Valencia, conquered by King James I the Conqueror in 1229 and 1232 respectively. Alfons I (1162-96), the first Count-King of the Crown of Aragon, issued *diners* and obols of copper and silver alloy in Barcelona and Aragon as well as in the county of Provence, all with designs of great iconographic simplicity. The *diners* issued in Barcelona **(146.1)** depict a cross over a pole between two rings: the sign or distinguishing emblem that the king used in his written documents. On the coins issued in Marseilles **(146.2)**, the effigy of the crowned king was rendered in a highly schematic manner.

In addition to issuing coins in Barcelona **(146.3, 146.4 & 146.5)** and in Aragon —in Jaca, to be precise— **(146.6)**, James I (1213-76) began minting coins in the recently conquered Valencia **(146.7)**. The bust of the crowned king was portrayed on all the coinage, surrounded by inscriptions that refer to the places of issue, namely *BARCINO*, but also *ARAGON* and *VALENCIE*. On the reverse side of the coins, in addition to the legend with the name of the king —*IACOBUS REX*—, different iconographic motifs were chosen to distinguish the coinage of each kingdom. Barcelona adopted a cross with rings, and dots in the quadrants, a design that has come down to modern times. Aragon established a patriarchal cross with two crosspieces, and Valencia, a tree surmounted by a cross.

The Count-Kings also continued minting coins the value and prestige of which was already established. In the domain of Montpellier —now under the vassalage of the Count-Kings— the minting of *diners melgoresos* continued (146.8). These were initially issued by the Counts of Melgueil, and their ancestral iconographic motifs remain unchanged.

SECTION XIX

The Ribagorça Workshop

EXHIBITED IN THIS SECTION are works attributed to the Ribagorça Workshop which form one of the most homogeneous groups of Catalan panel painting in the second half of the 13th century. All the pieces assembled here are part of this group —others will be mentioned later— and come from the area of the former county and bishopric of Ribagorça. The capital of the bishopric was the former episcopal town of Roda de Isábena or de Ribagorça, a diocese merged with the one in Lleida, to where the bishop moved in 1149. However, the old Cathedral of Roda continued to be classed as a cathedral and kept its own chapter.

These works from the Ribagorça Workshop share the same artistic characteristics, with bright colours and an anecdotal narrative style close to the Gothic, and also the same technique, remarkable for its backgrounds of stucco reliefwork which was then covered with silverleaf painted with yellow varnish (*colradura*), giving the pieces the appearance of gold and making the colour of the figures stand out. Many of the frontals that come from this workshop also include a narration of the lives and legends of the patron saints of their respective churches.

The current appearance of these works is very different from what it was originally —before the silverleaf deteriorated and caused much of the paint to fall off. They certainly must have looked like works made from precious metals. It is not surprising, then, that there was a great demand for them, the large number of works that have been preserved bearing this out. As for the motifs on the stucco background (fleur-de-lys or simple lozenges) within a rhomboidal reticule of dots, it has been argued that they must be identifying marks or emblems of the workshop, and, also, that the fleur-de lys motif is much later. In any case, all these aspects are open to question and must be studied further.

The narrative sense is very well developed on all the frontals produced by the Ribagorça Workshop, as is the taste for description and anecdote, as in the case of the parament in the scene of St. Martin on his deathbed on the *Frontal from Chía* **147**. Another example of this love of detail can be seen on the different shields of the two soldiers who guard the tower where St. Peter is imprisoned, found on the *Frontal from Boí* (149).

It is very likely that the artistic centre which produced these frontals sprang up in the region around the old Cathedral of Roda. On the whole, the preference has been to give the workshop the name of the geographic region rather than the name of the town, because no one knows for certain where it was located. The relationship that existed between the old Cathedral of Roda and the workshop that manufactured the frontals, and how it got its commissions, is also unknown. Nothing is known, either, about the internal organisation of the workshop, nor is it known if the master-painter John, who signed the *Frontal from Chía* —considered by some art historians as the archetype of the style— was the person in charge of the workshop or not. It appears, rather, that it may be that there were various painters in a group, one of whom was Master John, who would work with assistants. Another member of this workshop might have painted the figures of the *Frontal from Cardet* (IV, 66), a work which, when taken with the *Frontal from Rigatell, or Betesa* **148**, is one of the finest of this group.

Other works attributed to the Ribagorça Workshop are: the *Frontal from Sant Pere in Boí* (149), which is also exhibited here and has St. Peter at its centre, in a composition very similar to the one with St. Martin, who centres the painting on the *Frontal from Chía* **147**; the cross of unknown origin (150); the *Frontal from Sant Climent in Taüll* (V, 69), which has no central figure; the frontals from Sant Vicenç de Tresserra (Museu Diocesà de Lleida); and the Sacred Sepulchre (Museu Episcopal de Vic), which also comes from Sant Climent in Taüll. A reliquary casket conserved in Majorca is also attributed to this group; it may have come from the same Cathedral of Roda de Ribagorça.

147 *Altar frontal from Chía*

SECOND HALF OF THE 13TH CENTURY

THIS FRONTAL COMES from the Church of San Martín in Chía, located in the Benasque Valley in the region of Ribagorça (Aragon). It is signed by the painter, *'IOH(ANNE)S PINTOR ME FECIT'*, which makes this frontal unique in respect to other works from the Ribagorça Workshop. On the other hand, the fact that the frontal bears the painter's signature shows that this is a time in which the figure of the artist is beginning to be appreciated. Another important element —one that we also have referred to in the introduction to the section— is that the counterpane on St. Martin's deathbed has stripes in the colours of the Catalan-Aragonese flag, although here it does not appear to have an heraldic meaning. However, perhaps there was an heraldic meaning to the two small shields, now lacking colour, on the frame. This frontal, like the others from the workshop, lost parts of its paintwork when the silver that originally covered the background deteriorated.

The seated figure of St. Martin who centres the frontal is almost identical to the figure of St. Peter in the *Frontal from Boí* (149). St. Martin is portrayed as a bishop, wearing a mitre and holding a crozier while making a gesture of blessing with his right hand. His life and the miracles he performed are painted on the side panels. Above, on the left, St. Martin's act of charity is depicted: the saint sharing his cape with the poor man that the letters *('IHS')* identify with Jesus Christ. Below, one of his miracles is depicted, as well as the Virgin nursing the Holy Child, who, according to legend, appeared before St. Martin. Above, on the right, the mass of St. Martin or his second act of charity. Finally, in the last compartment, the devil makes one final effort to tempt the saint.

148 *Altar frontal from Rigatell*

SECOND HALF OF THE 13TH CENTURY

MOST OF THE HISTORIOGRAPHY concerning this frontal identifies it as the frontal from Betesa, when in reality it comes from the Hermitage and Sanctuary of the Virgin of Rigatell, which used to belong to the township of Betesa and today belongs to that of Areny de Noguera (Arén, Huesca). This frontal, along with the frontal from Cardet **(IV, 66)**, is one of the best works from the Ribagorça Workshop, as far as quality is concerned. The seated figure of the Virgin nursing the Holy Infant in the central compartment is the outstanding feature of the painting due to the harmonious beauty of her face, the proportions of her figure, and the delicate and detailed draughtsmanship of her attire. The episodes of Christ's infancy depicted are: the Annunciation; the Birth of Christ, above on the right; the Three Kings who have come to adore the Holy Child, in the lower compartment on the left; and in the compartment on the right, the announcement of Christ's birth to the Shepherds.

SECTION XX

The paintings from the palatine hall of San Pedro in Arlanza

IN THIS SECTION three fragments of mural painting are exhibited which are from the decoration of a room in the Monastery of San Pedro in Arlanza, Burgos, which was very important in the early Middle Ages.

Legend associates the origins of the Benedictine Monastery of San Pedro in Arlanza with Count Fernán González, who was entombed in this church in a sepulchre that is now conserved in the collegiate church of Covarrubias. The famous poem which recounts his deeds as the founder of the independent County of Castile was written in Arlanza. The monastery, cradle of the Crown of Castile, enjoyed the protection of its kings. The ruin and spoliation of the monastery began as a result of the disentailment of 1836. Its restoration was begun in 1989.

The paintings exhibited formed part of the decoration of a palatine chamber or hall for secular use, perhaps as a royal residence. This chamber is located on the first floor of the so-called Torre del Tesoro (Tower of the Treasure), that is located on the southeast side of the church, on the east side of the cloister, just above the space where the chapter house of the monastery was. In the 18th century, with the construction of a Neo-classical cloister, and a monumental staircase built to join the two floors of the tower, the west wall of the hall was torn down. Thus, the frescoes that have been preserved come from the other walls. In addition to the paintings in the Museum (the ones exhibited and the ones in the reserve collection), the The Cloisters Museum in New York, a section of the Metropolitan Museum of Art, and the Fogg Art Museum of the University of Harvard conserve other paintings from the same group.

The decoration on the walls of the hall was organised with a central band, some two metres in height, which contained the depiction of mythical animals of a monumental character, placed either side of the windows in bilateral symmetry, some of them in a somewhat defensive attitude. Above this band, which occupied the greater part of the decorated surface, there were

ornamental borders with geometric and plant motifs. Beneath the large frieze with the mythical animals there was a frieze of lesser height with scenes that appeared to have come from a book of fables, with dancing animals, animals playing musical instruments, birds with human faces looking at each other, as well as other people and animals.

The largest exhibited mural —from the south wall— contains the figure of a magnificent monumental griffin, a mythical animal with the lower half of its body a lion's, and the upper, an eagle's, and with its front talons rampant, which appears to defend the chamber from whatever sought to enter through the double window set in that side of the wall. Behind, there is a tree full of fruit which is perhaps intended to represent the sacred tree or the Tree of Life which griffins used to defend, according to a tradition of Oriental origin incorporated into Western imagery. There was a badly-preserved frieze below the griffin, from which the Museum possesses a pair of apes, not displayed. On the other side of the window, there had been a winged dragon, also in an attitude of defending the chamber from possible intruders (The Cloisters).

The castle on the other mural, which comes from the north wall, may have an heraldic meaning: the castle on the arms of the Kings of Castile. It was placed over the arch of the doorway which gave onto a small chamber, a kind of hiding-place, built right behind the south apse and located on the floor above the sacristy. In that respect, we may ask whether the name of the tower, 'the Tower of the Treasure', the mythical guardian animals which symbolically defended access to the chamber, and the small hiding-place could have a special meaning, or if this is a mere coincidence. In any event, there had been another imaginary creature —a kind of monumental bird or hybrid being, difficult to identify— beside the doorway with the depiction of the castle but with its back to it and facing the window. It is now in the Fogg Art Museum. This animal flanked a small round-arched window, in whose spandrel the third of the displayed fragments was found: a long-legged bird-like animal with two antennae, whose body fits perfectly into the space where it is inserted.

The Museum possesses another two fragments from Arlanza not yet mentioned. Both of them are from the east wall: one is a large quadruped —the head is not preserved— that used to flank a window. Behind it, there is an oriental-type domed building. The other fragment comes from the right spandrel of the window and contains a short-legged bird with a long body. Near this bird, and opposite the quadruped, there was a magnificent lion (The Cloisters).

The Arlanza paintings are as vigourous in style —especially the large animals— as they are delicate, in their realization, with fine cross-hatching which outlines or emphasises the details (see the tree and the griffin) and a muted range of colours. These are works of great skill. These monumental paintings from Arlanza have been linked to the ones from the chapter house at Sigena which are so intensely Byzantine. However, it is more likely that the relationship to Sigena is of another kind. The two groups are court paintings: their creation depended on the royal patronage of Castile and Aragon, and this fact underlies the great artistic quality of both. Other iconographic similarities between the bestiary from Arlanza and Sigena exist, and must be attributed to the same pictorial tradition, or at least to common or closely related sources that the particular artists must have used. In all likelihood, these sources would be related to English illuminated manuscripts from *c.* 1200. The same relationship can be established regarding a miniature in which there is a lion very similar to the one from Arlanza, the former being added to the chartulary *Tumbo A* in Santiago de Compostela between 1189 and 1208, which, furthermore would corroborate the dating of the Arlanza paintings as being *c.* 1200.

SECTION XXI

The paintings from the chapter house of Sigena

IN THE LAST section, the structure of the chapter house of the Aragonese nunnery at Santa María in Sigena (Huesca) —connected to the order of the Hospital of St. John of Jerusalem— has been reproduced with as much faithfulness to the original as possible. This rectangular nave opened onto the cloister via four small arches. The hall was covered with a flat coffered ceiling supported by five large blunt arcades.

The murals that once decorated the Sigena chapter house constituted one of the most outstanding works of the age and the most representative example of monumental painting in the Neo-Byzantine style of the year 1200 (see section XIII).

During the Spanish Civil War in 1936, the burning of the nunnery caused irreversible damage. The magnificent Mudejar coffered ceiling was burnt, and the paintings on the north and east walls were irreparably lost, as well as the ones on the north face of the first of the blunt arches. Furthermore, the paintings that were saved lost the luminosity and splendour of their original polychromy. Due to the chemical action of the fire, the blues turned black and the greens, brown, and the rest of the colours became opaque and muddy. Only one of the arches that had led to the cloister —which had been walled in since ancient times— escaped the direct action of the fire, but not of the smoke, hence its colours are somewhat better-preserved.

The arch paintings were removed in the year the fire took place, by a team of specialists sent from Barcelona; this same team also took charge of transferring the frescoes to canvas and restoring them. Then, using the photographs taken before the fire, they drew the missing scenes and the decorated borders on a neutral background. In 1940, the now restored paintings arrived at the Museum. The paintings on the north wall were left exposed to all weathers for a number of years. It was not until 1960 that they were removed from the wall by the specialists from the restoration workshop of the Barcelona Art Museums.

Before starting the new installation of the chapter house in 1995, and with the aim of avoiding any risks during the removal and their new location on the walls of the Museum, the extremely fragile Sigena paintings have been consolidated strengthened throughout. When this work was undertaken, the question was posed of whether it was convenient to eliminate the drawings —realized prior to the arrival of the frescoes in the Museum—, that fill in the gaps of the original paintings. Finally, it was decided to keep these reconstructions, at least until it is possible to undertake a complete restoration of the paintings. This decision was taken because this type of restoration —an historical reconstruction— aids understanding without inflicting damage to the original work. Moreover, it is easy to tell the difference between the authentic paintings and the drawings. Despite the irreversible damage that the fire caused to the Sigena murals, the mastery of its extraordinary draughtsmanship can still be distinguished, as can the beauty of the modelling of the figures, the composition of the scenes, as well as the wealth of ornamental subjects and those from the bestiary.

The Byzantine influence, which is so strong in these paintings, has been attributed unanimously by historiography to English artists who had worked on illuminated manuscripts, in particular to the atelier of the *Morgan Leaf*'s author (Pierpont Morgan Library, New York) from the *Winchester Bible* (Winchester Cathedral). Apparently, these painters were at the nunnery then, possibly having worked in Sicily before their arrival. Therefore, they might have been acquainted with the mosaics in the palatine chapel of Palermo, and in the Cathedrals of Cefalú and Monreale, where they probably learnt their skills and

became impregnated with this highly powerful Byzantine style (see section XIII). Later, they must have worked on the *Winchester Bible*, and lastly in Sigena.

The pictorial programme which covers all the feasible surfaces of the chapter house is comprised of three distinct and interrelated cycles. Twenty episodes from the Old Testament were depicted on the lateral faces of the arches. The New Testament was painted on the perimetral walls of the hall. The third area is the one with Christ's ancestry, occupying the intradoses of the arches as a link between the Old and the New Testament. Moreover, as *marginalia*, both a real and imaginary bestiary was portrayed amidst a rich and exuberant flora.

The episodes from the Old Testament focussed on the repeated Sin of man. The scenes occupy the two faces of the arches, with an episode in each of the spandrels. The episodes are taken from the Books of Genesis and Exodus, and the last two are from Numbers and First Book of Samuel. Eighteen of the twenty episodes that existed —four on each arch— have been preserved: the paintings on the face of the first arch, where the Creation of Adam and Eve had been depicted, were lost in the fire. Today, the cycle begins on the south side of the first of the arches —the one furthest from the exit— with the scene where God shows the Paradise to Adam and Eve. The depiction of the original Sin is on the other side of the arch; the next one shows the Expulsion from the Garden of Eden and an apocryphal episode often painted in English art, in which the Angel teaches Adam to work the land. On the other face of the arch —the second— there is a representation of the labours of Adam and Eve, and another of the

Offerings of Cain and Abel. Next, on the third arch, there is the Slaying of Abel: Cain kills his brother with a blow from an ass's jaw, according to an old English tradition. On the other spandrel on this same face arch, Noah builds the ark. On the other face of the arch— in a magnificent scene with a very strong Byzantine influence— we see the Entering of the animals into Noah's ark and the dove's return after the Flood with people drowning beneath the waves. On the fourth arch the Drunkenness of Noah, and the Sacrifice of Isaac can be discerned. On the other face of the arch, Pharaoh's army drowns in the Red Sea, and Aaron shows the Jewish people the Pillar of Fire. On the fifth and last arch, Moses receives the Tables of the Law, in which God shows His face on the burning bush. At His side birds hang from a tree by their beaks (see table below). On the other end of the arch, the Adoration of the Golden Calf is shown. Lastly, on the other face of this arch are Moses drawing water from the rock, and the Anointing of David by Samuel.

The New Testament, or story of Salvation, occupied the perimetral walls of the hall. It began on the north wall with the Annunciation and the Birth of Jesus, now lost. On the east wall, there were displayed diverse scenes from the life and Passion of Christ, as well as the miracle of the Raising of Lazarus. The cycle ends on the south wall with the Flagellation; the Crucifixion, and the three Marys at the Tomb of Christ. This last is an allegory of the Resurrection of Jesus. The iconography of the Crucifixion is especially noteworthy in spite of the fact that the paintings are very deteriorated. On the arms of the cross, there are two angels,

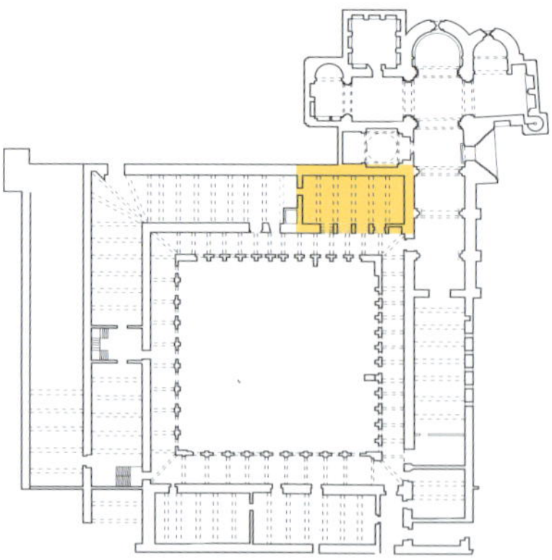

Paintings conserved in the MNAC

and below, two more angels accompanying two female figures who can be identified as the Church and the Synagogue; they are portrayed from the waist up as in the Byzantine tradition. The figure of the Church is located on the left: her covered hands carry a chalice to collect the blood of Christ. Below her are Mary and John and the Faithful. The figure of the Synagogue is on the other side; below, the temple of Jerusalem and the Jews can be made out.

The intradoses of the first two arches are occupied by portraits of Christ's ancestors, according to St. Matthew, and on the three last we can see Luke's version of Christ's genealogy. Only a selection of the ancestors mentioned in the biblical text could be portrayed since the available space was limited: a maximum of sixteen portraits could be placed on each arch. The portraits were identified by inscriptions which did not survive.

The genealogy of Christ by Matthew (Matthew 1, 1-16) on the first two arches (the ones opposite the exit) began on the opposite side to the cloister with the portrait of Isaac (not preserved), the son of Abraham, and reached until a few generations before Joseph, Mary's husband. Each compartment includes the figures of the father and his son. Below them, there were epigraphs specifying the relationship (*'...autem genuit ...'* 'he begat'), but almost all of them have been lost. The portraits in this genealogy that are worth noting are the ones of Jesse and King David, who wears a crown and holds a sceptre; this can be seen on the lower part of the first arcade, near the arch that used to lead to the cloister.

The genealogy from Luke (Luke 3, 23-38), which begins in the Bible with Joseph, Mary's husband, occupied the other three arches. The first three portraits of this genealogy —beginning on the third arch opposite the cloister— have not been preserved. The fourth is Jannai; above him is the remarkable portrait of his father, Joseph, and above him Matthat. The portrait of the first man, Adam (not preserved), was on the fourth arch, beside the Resurrection.

Finally, on the upper part of the arches, as *marginalia*, a complementary cycle unfolds depicting a rich bestiary amidst exuberant vegetation. The presence of these animals sometimes has an implicit meaning, or they may call attention to other biblical episodes close by. Richly elaborated animals taken from bestiaries and from fables are at times shown face-to-face: lions, griffins, strange birds with foliate tails, deer, dragons and also centaurs. Less common is the depiction of a fable reproduced in English bestiaries from the beginning of the 13th century, the so-called *Barnacle Goose*, or the tree of hanging birds, according to the description Gerald of Wales made in his *Hibernian Topograph*y in 1188. There are earlier non-English illustrations and literary references from the 11th century, such as the *Rodes Bible*, from the Ripoll scriptorium (Bibliothèque Nationale, Paris) and in texts by Petrus Damianus, a Reformer and Doctor of the Church. In any case, it is thought that the manner of depicting this fable at Sigena is based on English bestiaries.

The paintings of the chapter house in Sigena must be dated a little before the year 1200 because of their style and iconography. The most recent studies argue that they could have been carried out between the years 1190 and 1194.

The nunnery of Santa Maria in Sigena was founded in 1187 by Queen Sancha, the daughter of Alfonso VII of Castile and wife of King Alfons I of Catalonia (II of Aragon), called the Chaste. From the time she became a widow in 1196 until her death in 1208, Queen Sancha lived in retirement in Sigena where, in 1213, her son King Pere the Catholic (who died at Muret in 1213 and had been a great protector of the nunnery), was buried.

List of works

1. APSE FROM SANT PERE IN LA SEU D'URGELL. First half of the 12th century. Fresco. 705 x 565 x 300 cm. From the Church of Sant Pere (now Sant Miquel), belonging to the episcopal group of La Seu d'Urgell (Alt Urgell). Acquisition, 1919-23. MNAC/MAC 15867

2. ALTAR FROM SANT SERNI DE TAVÈRNOLES. 12th century. Tempera on wood. Frontal: 118 x 218 cm (MNAC/MAC 15786); sides: 120 x 95 cm (MNAC/MAC 64003) and 122 x 93 cm (MNAC/MAC 64006). From the Monastery of Sant Serni de Tavèrnoles (Les Valls de Valira, Alt Urgell). Acquisition, 1907 and acquisition of the Muntadas Collection, 1956. MNAC/MAC 15786, 64003, 64006

3. ALTAR FRONTAL FROM LA SEU D'URGELL, ALSO KNOWN AS THE APOSTLES FRONTAL. First half of the 12th century. Tempera on wood. 102 x 151 cm. From a church belonging to the bishopric of La Seu d'Urgell. Acquisition, 1905. MNAC/MAC 15803

4. ALTAR FRONTAL FROM IX. First half of the 12th century. Tempera on wood. 92 x 157 cm. From the Church of Sant Martí in Ix/Hix (La Guingueta d'Ix/Bourg-Madame, Cerdagne). Acquisition of the Bosch i Barrau Collection, 1889. MNAC/MAC 15802

5. PRE-ROMANESQUE ALTAR. Reutilised as a holy water stoup. 10th century. Stone. 59 x 35 x 35 cm. From a church near Cardona (Bages). Former collection of the Museo Provincial de Antigüedades in Barcelona. MNAC/MAC 10000

6. THE CUBELLS CHRIST. 13th century. Tempera on wood carving with polychromy in tempera (the current polychromy is later). 67 x 19 x 14.2 cm. From the Church of Santa Maria in Cubells Castle (Noguera). On permanent loan from the Ministerio de Cultura, 1985. MNAC/MAC 122672

7. THE PRUNERES VIRGIN. Second half of the 12th century. Wood carving with traces of polychromy in tempera. 153 x 23 x 19 cm. From the Hermitage of Santa Bàrbara de Pruneres (Montagut de Fluvià, Garrotxa). Acquisition of the Plandiura Collection, 1932. MNAC/MAC 4386

8. THE MOROR CHRIST. *c.* 1180. Cast bronze, engraved and gilded. 19.3 x 19 x 3.5 cm. From the Church of Sant Miquel de Moror (Sant Esteve de la Sarga, Pallars Jussà). Acquisition, 1920. MNAC/MAC 12095

9. THE ORIGINS OF CATALAN COINAGE

9.1 Luis the Pious, *Diner* (814840). Silver. 1.62 g, 19 mm. MNAC/GNC 62805

9.2 *Diner* in imitation of a Carolingian *denier* with Charles' name, minted in Barcelona. 10th century. Silver. 1.25 g, 18 mm. MNAC/GNC 15145

9.3 *Diner* from the bishopric of Vic, attributed to the Bishop Guadamir (948-957). Silver. 1.01 g, 14 mm. MNAC/GNC 15254

9.4 Hisham II, *Dinar* (AH 366-403/AD 976-1013), minted in Al-Andalus. Gold. 3.34 g, 22 mm. MNAC/GNC 37925

9.5 Ramon Berenguer I, *Mancús* (1035-1076), minted in Barcelona. Gold. 3.42 g, 22 mm. MNAC/GNC 15150

10. ISLAMIC TOMBSTONE WITH AN EPITAPH FROM AMTA BEN HARUN BEN IAHDAH. 1011. Marble. 91 x 43 x 5 cm. From Cordoba. Acquisition, 1972. MNAC/MAC 108260

11. CHRISTIAN TOMBSTONE WITH AN EPITAPH FROM *LEVANTO*. Probably by *Gomarellus*. 976. Marble. 34 x 40 x 8 cm. Probably from Barcelona. Former collection of the Museo Provincial de Antigüedades in Barcelona. MNAC/MAC 14302

12. HEBREW TOMBSTONE WITH AN EPITAPH FROM ABRAHAM. 9th or 10th century. Marble. 36 x 32 x 10 cm. On permanent loan from the Museu d'Història de la Ciutat in Barcelona (MHC 1094), 1995. MNAC/MAC 200816

13. VISIGOTHIC PLAQUE. Second half of the 6th century. Marble. 44.5 x 46.5 x 8 cm. Probably from the Cathedral of Barcelona. Guift of Francesc Torres to the Museo Provincial de Antigüedades in Barcelona. MNAC/MAC 9994

14. VISIGOTHIC CAPITAL. 7th century. Stone. 41 x 41 x 40 cm. From Cordoba. Admission, 1934. MNAC/MAC 22993

15. CALIPHAL CAPITAL. First half of the 10th century. Marble. 22 x 21.5 x 21.5 cm. From Madinat-al-Zahara (Cordoba). Gift of Manuel Trallero, 1982. MNAC/MAC 122203

16. ABACUS FROM A CALIPHAL CAPITAL. First half of the 10th century. Marble. 20 x 34 x 32 cm. From Madinat-al-Zahara (Cordoba). Acquisition, 1971. MNAC/MAC 108261

17. CALIPHAL CAPITAL. Second half of the 10th century. Marble. 28 x 23 x 24 cm. From Cordoba. Gift of Lluís Barbié, 1985. MNAC/MAC 122673

18. EMIRAL OR CALIPHAL CAPITAL. First third of the 10th century. Marble. 24 x 23 x 23 cm. From Cordoba. Gift of Artur Ramon, 1982. MNAC/MAC 122204

19. CALIPHAL CAPITAL. *c.* 964-65 (According to the inscription from the period of the Caliph Al-Hakam II [961-76]). Marble. 41.5 x 36 x 36 cm. From the Alcazar of Cordoba. Gift of the Claretian Fathers of Barcelona, 1977. MNAC/MAC 122001

20. CAPITAL FROM CASTELLTERÇOL. End of the 10th century. Stone. 32.8 x 32.5 x 32.5 cm. From Castellterçol (Vallès Oriental). Acquisition, 1974. MNAC/MAC 113731

21. ISLAMIC PLAQUE. 11th century. Alabaster. 20 x 22 x 5 cm. From a royal palace in Toledo. Acquisition, 1921. MNAC/MAC 24194

22. IMPOSTS FROM THE CATHEDRAL OF BARCELONA. 11th century. Stone. 27.5 x 70 x 43 cm (MNAC/MAC 14397) and 27.5 x 40 x 43 cm (MNAC/MAC 14398). From the Romanesque Cathedral of Barcelona. Former collection of the Museo Provincial de Antigüedades in Barcelona. MNAC/MAC 14397, 14398

23. CAPITAL AND IMPOST FROM ÀGER. 11th century. Stone. 30 x 33 x 37 cm (MNAC/MAC 24002) and 12 x 43 x 43 cm (MNAC/MAC 49368). From the Church of Sant Pere in Àger (Noguera). Admission before 1926. MNAC/MAC 24002, 49368

24. IMPOST FRAGMENT. 11th or 12th century. Marble. 17 x 41.5 x 23 cm. Probably from Roussillon. On permanent loan, 1984. MNAC/MAC 122500

25. CAPITAL FROM SANT PERE DE RODES. 11th or 12th century. Stone. 25.5 x 25 x 33 cm. From the Abbey of Sant Pere de Rodes (El Port de la Selva, Alt Empordà). Gift of Macari Golferichs, 1921. MNAC/MAC 24114

26. PAINTINGS FROM THE CHURCH OF SANT JOAN IN BOÍ. *c.* 1100. Fresco. The Stoning of St. Steven: 184 x 353 cm (MNAC/MAC 15953); Paradise and Hell: 188 x 357 cm (MNAC/MAC 15951); Falconer: 142 x 146 cm (MNAC/MAC 15862). From the Church of Sant Joan in Boí (La Vall de Boí, Alta Ribagorça). Acquisition, 1920-22. MNAC/MAC 15796, 15822, 15862, 15951-15956, 200423-200441, 200817

27. ALTAR STONE FROM CASTELLET, ALSO KNOWN AS LES MASUQUES ALTAR STONE. 10th century. Reutilised marble. 30 x 117 x 74 cm. From the Church of Sant Esteve in Castellet, near Les Masuques (Castellet i la Gornal, Alt Penedès). On permanent loan from the Museu Diocesà de Barcelona. MNAC/MAC 122012

28. CERDANYA CHRIST. 12th century. Wood carving. 64 x 67 x 10 cm. From Cerdanya. Former collection of the Barcelona Museums. MNAC/MAC 113157

29. THE ESCALÓ CHRIST. 12th century. Wood carving with traces of polychromy in tempera. 74 x 71 x 14 cm. From Escaló (La Guingueta d'Àneu, Pallars Sobirà). Accession, 1958. MNAC/MAC 64960

30. SIDE APSES FROM PEDRET. End of the 11th century. Fresco. South apse: 325 x 315 x 325 cm (MNAC/MAC 15973); north apse: 300 x 275 x 250 cm (MNAC/MAC 22991-22992). From the apsidioles of the Church of Sant Quirze in Pedret (Cercs, Berguedà). Acquisition, 1922. MNAC/MAC 15973, 22991-22992

31. APOSTLES FROM ÀGER: THADDAEUS AND JAMES. *c.* 1100. Fresco. 280 x 145 cm. From the central apse of the Church of Sant Pere in Àger (Noguera). On permanent loan, 1958. MNAC/MAC 65467

32. COINAGE OF THE COUNTS AND BISHOPS

A. COUNTY COINAGE

32.1 Berenguer Ramon I *Diner,* (1018-35), minted in Barcelona. Silver. 0.33 g, 13 mm. MNAC/GNC 302277

32.2 Ramón Berenguer IV *Diner,* (1131-62), minted in Girona. Silver. 0.37 g, 15 mm. MNAC/GNC 15191

32.3 *Diner* from the county of Besalú, attributed to Guillem I (1020-52). Silver. 0.88 g, 14 mm. MNAC/GNC 11153

B. EPISCOPAL COINAGE

32.4 *Diner* from the bishopric of Vic, attributed to Bishop Oliba (1017-46). Silver. 0.99 g, 15 mm. MNAC/GNC 10730

32.5 & 32.6 *Diner* from the bishopric of Vic, attributed to Bishop Berenguer Sunifred (1073-99). Silver. 0.96 g, 15 mm. (MNAC/GNC 10732) and 1.03 g, 16 mm. (MNAC/GNC 15263)

32.7 *Diner* from the bishopric of Vic, Girona. 11th century. Silver. 0.30 g, 13 mm. MNAC/GNC 15183

32.8 *Diner* from the bishopric of Girona. 11th century. Silver. 0.40 g, 12 mm. MNAC/GNC 15177

33. CROZIER: St. Michael Killing the Dragon. Limoges, *c.* 1230-40. *Champlevé* enamelling on gilded and engraved cast copper. Cast figures in full relief. 33 x 7 cm (volute diameter) and 3.5 cm (knob diameter). Bequest of Santiago Espona, 1958. MNAC/MAC 65523

34. CROZIER. Limoges, *c.* 1230-40. *Champlevé* enamelling on gilded cast copper. 34 x 11 cm (volute diameter) and 8 cm (knob diameter). Bequest of Santiago Espona, 1958. MNAC/MAC 65522

35. CROZIER. The Annunciation. Limoges, *c.* 1240. *Champlevé* enamelling on gilded and engraved cast copper. Cast figures in full relief. 37.5 x 14 cm (volute diameter) and 11 cm (knob diameter). Bequest of Santiago Espona, 1958. MNAC/MAC 65524

36. ENAMELLED PLAQUE: Sanctified Bishop. 13th century. Embossed copper with *champlevé* enamelling. 22 x 11.4 x 2 cm. Acquisition of the Plandiura Collection, 1932. MNAC/MAC 4568

37. APSE FROM SANTA MARIA D'ÀNEU. End of the 11th century. Fresco. 760 x 460 x 240 cm. From the Church of Santa Maria d'Àneu (La Guingueta d'Àneu, Àneu Valley, Pallars Sobirà). Acquisition, 1919-23. MNAC/MAC 15874

38. APSE FROM EL BURGAL. End of the 11th century. Fresco. 720 x 470 x 500 cm. From the Church of Sant Pere in El Burgal (La Guingueta d'Àneu, Àneu Valley, Pallars Sobirà). Acquisition of the Plandiura Collection, 1932. MNAC/MAC 113138

39. THE DONORESS OF SANT PERE IN ESTERRI D'ÀNEU. Second half of the 12th century. Fresco. 165 x 67 x 28 cm. From the old church of Sant Pere in Esterri d'Àneu (Àneu Valley, Pallars Sobirà). Acquisition of the Plandiura Collection, 1932. MNAC/MAC 4530

40. THE ORCAU APOSTLES. First half of the 12th century. Fresco. 172 x 186 cm. From the apse of Santa Maria in Orcau Castle (Isona i Conca Dellà, Pallars Jussà). Acquisition of the Plandiura Collection, 1932. MNAC/MAC 4532

41. PAINTINGS FROM ARGOLELL. First half of the 12th century. Fresco. Mary: 70 x 135 cm (MNAC/MAC 4536); Apostles: 123 x 129 cm (MNAC/MAC 4537); window: 104 x 76 cm (MNAC/MAC 4538). From the apse of Santa Eugènia in Argolell (Les Valls de Valira, Alt Urgell). Acquisition of the Plandiura Collection, 1932. MNAC/MAC 4536, 4537, 4538

42. SOUTH APSE AND COLUMN OF THE CENTRAL APSE FROM MUR. *c.* 1150. Fresco. Apse: 440 x 490 x 165 cm (MNAC/MAC 68710) and column: 279 x 29 cm (MNAC/MAC 68711). From the Church of Santa Maria in Mur (Castell de Mur, Pallars Jussà). On permanent loan, 1961. MNAC/MAC 68710, 68711

43. APSE FROM MARMELLAR. 11th or 12th century. Fresco. 480 x 355 x 300 cm. From the chapel of Sant Miquel in Marmellar Castle (El Montmell, Baix Penedès). Acquisition, 1962. MNAC/MAC 71998

44. APSE FROM ESTERRI DE CARDÓS. Second half of the 12th century. Fresco. 610 x 430 x 370 cm. From the Church of Sant Pau in Esterri de Cardós (Cardós Valley, Pallars Sobirà). Acquisition, 1919-23. MNAC/MAC 15970

45. ALTAR FRONTAL FROM ESTERRI DE CARDÓS. 1225 (according to the inscription). Stucco relief, formerly varnished with *colradura* and tempera on wood. 108 x 161 cm. From the Church of Sant Pau in Esterri de Cardós (Cardós Valley, Pallars Sobirà). Acquisition, 1911. MNAC/MAC 15889

46. APSE FROM GINESTARRE. Second half of the 12th century. Fresco. 580 x 365 x 250 cm. From the Church of Santa Maria in Ginestarre (Esterri de Cardós, Cardós Valley, Pallars Sobirà). Acquisition, 1919-23 and 1964. MNAC/MAC 15971

47. BALDACHIN FROM TOST. *c.* 1200. Tempera on wood. 177 x 175 cm. Probably from the Church of Sant Martí in Tost (Ribera d'Urgellet, Alt Urgell). Acquisition of the Plandiura Collection, 1932. MNAC/MAC 3905

48. ALTAR FRONTAL FROM BENAVENT. End of the 13th century. Wood carving with polychromy in tempera (the current polychromy is later). 84 x 144 cm. From the Church of Santa Margarida in Benavent (Isona i Conca Dellà, Pallars Jussà). Acquisition of the Plandiura Collection, 1932. MNAC/MAC 3914

49. THE SO-CALLED ALTAR FRONTAL FROM ESQUIUS. Second half of the 12th century. Tempera on wood. 96 x 132 cm. Esquius has never been identified as a place name. Bequest of Santiago Espona, 1958. MNAC/MAC 65502

50. CHRIST FROM CABDELLA. 12th or 13th century. Wood carving. Christ: 218 x 180 x 25.5 cm and cross: 227 x 179 x 3.5 cm. From the Church of Sant Vicenç in Cabdella (La Torre de Cabdella, Pallars Jussà). Acquisition of the Plandiura Collection, 1932. MNAC/MAC 3936

51. CROSS FROM BAGERGUE. *c.* 1200. Tempera on wood. 126 x 98 cm. From the Church of Sant Feliu in Bagergue (Alt Aran, Val d'Aran). Acquisition of the Plandiura Collection, 1932. MNAC/MAC 3937

52. MAJESTY FROM ÉLLER. Second half of the 12th century (modern cross). Wood carving with polychromy in tempera. 83 x 85 x 15 cm. Probably from Éller (Bellver de Cerdanya, Baixa Cerdanya). Acquisition of the Plandiura Collection, 1932. MNAC/MAC 49366

53. CALVARY FROM TRAGÓ DE NOGUERA. Second half of the 13th century. Wood carving with polychromy in tempera. Christ: 60 x 55.5 x 13.5 cm; cross: 148 x 81 x 9 cm. Probably from Tragó de Noguera (Os de Balaguer, Noguera). Acquisition, 1912. MNAC/MAC 15887

54. CHRIST IN MAJESTY FROM BASARÁN. 12th century. Wood carving with traces of polychromy in tempera. 56 x 20 x 10.5 cm. From Basarán (Huesca). Acquisition of the Plandiura Collection, 1932. MNAC/MAC 3927

55. FRAGMENT OF AN ITALIAN CROSS. Second half of the 13th century. Tempera on wood. 32 x 25 cm. Probably from the region of Las Marcas (Central Italy). Acquisition of the Plandiura Collection, 1932. MNAC/MAC 5215

56. CHRIST. *c.* 1180. Cast bronze, engraved and gilded. 22 x 21.5 x 4 cm. Probably from Cerdanya. Acquisition of the Plandiura Collection, 1932. MNAC/MAC 4553

57. CHRIST ON THE CROSS. Limoges, *c.* 1190. *Champlevé* enamelling on gilded and engraved cast copper. 28.6 x 19 x 0.5 cm. Bequest of Santiago Espona, 1958. MNAC/MAC 65508

58. BOOKBINDING PLATE: Crucifixion. Limoges, *c.* 1190-1200. *Champlevé* enamelling on cast copper; the heads in relief. 23.5 x 10.5 cm. Bequest of Santiago Espona, 1958. MNAC/MAC 65558

59. CHÂSSE: Resurrection. Limoges, *c.* 1220. *Champlevé* enamelling on gilded cast copper over wood core. Heads in relief. 30 x 22 x 8 cm. Bequest of Santiago Espona, 1958. MNAC/MAC 65530

60. VIRGIN. Limoges, second third of the 13th century. Gilded cast copper. 22.5 x 8 x 4.8 cm. Bequest of Santiago Espona, 1958. MNAC/MAC 66057

61. VIRGIN FROM GER. Second half of the 12th. Wood carving with polychromy in tempera. 52.5 x 20.5 x 14.5 cm. From the Church of Santa Coloma in Ger (Baixa Cerdanya). Bequest of Santiago Espona, 1958. MNAC/MAC 65503

62. VIRGIN. 13th century. Wood carving with polychromy in tempera. 54 x 16 x 17.5 cm. Acquisition of the Plandiura Collection, 1932. MNAC/MAC 3921

63. VIRGIN. 13th century. Wood carving with traces of polychromy in tempra. 64 x 20 x 14 cm. Acquisition of the Plandiura Collection, 1932. MNAC/MAC 4397

64. VIRGIN FROM MATADARS. Second half of the 12th century. Wood carving with traces of polychromy in tempera. 60 x 33 x 28 cm. From the Church of Santa Maria in Matadars or El Marquet (El Pont de Vilomara, Bages). Acquisition of the Plandiura Collection, 1932. MNAC/MAC 4392

65. ALTAR FRONTAL FROM ALÓS D'ISIL. First quarter of the 13th century. Stucco relief and tempera on wood. 106 x 161 cm. Probably from Alós d'Isil (Alt Àneu, Pallars Sobirà). Acquisition, 1907. MNAC/MAC 15834

66. ALTAR FRONTAL FROM CARDET. Second half of the 13th century. Tempera on wood with stucco relief formerly varnished with *colradura*. 96 x 160 cm. From the Church of Santa Maria in Cardet (La Vall de Boí, Alta Ribagorça). Acquisition of the Plandiura Collection, 1932. MNAC/MAC 3903

67. ALTAR FRONTAL FROM MOSOLL. Middle of the 13th century. Tempera on wood. 100 x 168 cm. From the Church of Santa Maria in Mosoll (Das, Baixa Cerdanya). Acquisition, 1906. MNAC/MAC 15788

68. PAINTINGS FROM SANT CLIMENT IN TAÜLL. *c.* 1123. Fresco. Central apse: 770 x 420 x 590 cm (MNAC/MAC 15966); angel: 136 x 77 cm (MNAC/MAC 15860); seated figure: 131 x 116 cm (MNAC/MAC 200752); window: 68 x 33 cm (MNAC/MAC 113142). From the Church of Sant Climent in Taüll (La Vall de Boí, Alta Ribagorça). Acquisition, 1923 and 1960. MNAC/MAC 15806, 15860, 15966-15968, 22996, 113142, 200752

69. ALTAR FRONTAL FROM SANT CLIMENT IN TAÜLL. Second half of the 13th century. Tempera on wood with stucco relief formerly varnished with *colradura*. 93 x 169 cm. From the Church of Sant Climent in Taüll (La Vall de Boí, Alta Ribagorça). Acquisition of the Plandiura Collection, 1932. MNAC/MAC 3908

70. PRESBYTERIAL BENCH FROM SANT CLIMENT IN TAÜLL. 12th or 13th century. Carved and openworked wood. 260 x 160 x 62 cm. From the Church of Sant Climent in Taüll (La Vall de Boí, Alta Ribagorça). Acquisition, 1920. MNAC/MAC 15898

71. LIPSANOTHÈQUE FROM SANT CLIMENT IN TAÜLL. End of the 11th century. Wood with polychromy in tempera. 12.5 x 8.5 cm. From the Church of Sant Climent in Taüll (La Vall de Boí, Alta Ribagorça). Bequest of Martí Estany, 1937. MNAC/MAC 37927

72. '*DE PETRVS*' CROSS. Castile or León, 1122 (according to the inscription). Bronze with encrusted rock crystals. 47 x 39 x 4 cm. Acquisition, 1906. MNAC/MAC 12180

73. CENSER. Catalonia, second quarter of the 12th century. *Champlevé* enamelling on gilded and engraved cast copper. 13 x 13.5 cm (diameter). Acquisition of the Plandiura Collection, 1932. MNAC/MAC 4581

74. CANDLESTICKS. Burgos or Silos, *c.* 1200. *Champlevé* enamelling on engraved and embossed cast copper. 18.5 x 12.4 cm (MNAC/MAC 65551); 17 x 11.4 cm (MNAC/MAC 65553). Bequest of Santiago Espona, 1958. MNAC/MAC 65551, 65553

75. CHÂSSE OF ST. STEPHEN. Limoges, *c.* 1210-20. *Champlevé* enamelling on gilded and engraved cast copper over a wood core. 16 x 13 x 5 cm. Bequest of Santiago Espona, 1958. MNAC/MAC 65526

76. CIBORIUM. Limoges, *c.* 1220-40. *Champlevé* enamelling on embosed, gilded and engraved cast copper. 31 x 14.5 cm (diameter). Acquisition of the Plandiura Collection, 1932. MNAC/MAC 4600

77. PYX. Limoges, *c.* 1220-40. *Champlevé* enamelling on gilded and engraved cast copper. 12.5 x 7.3 cm (diameter). Probably from the Church in Ars (Les Valls de Valira, Alt Urgell). Acquisition, 1906. MNAC/MAC 12107

78. INCENSE BOAT. Limoges, second half of the 13th century. *Champlevé* enamelling on gilded and engraved cast copper. 4.5 x 19 x 8.2 cm. Acquisition of the Plandiura Collection, 1932. MNAC/MAC 4567

79. BOOKBINDING PLATE. Christ in Majesty. Limoges, *c.* 1190-1200. *Champlevé* enamelling on cast copper; cast heads. 24 x 11 cm. Bequest of Santiago Espona, 1958. MNAC/MAC 65560

80. HOLY WATER STOUP. 12th or 13th century. Stone. Base: 76 x 29 x 29 cm; receptacle: 28 cm. Acquisition of the Plandiura Collection, 1932. MNAC/MAC 5298

81. THE SO-CALLED BALDACHIN FROM TOSES. First third of the 13th century. Tempera on wood. 488 x 238 x 216 cm. According to the traditional version this comes from the Church of Sant Cristòfol in Toses (Ribes Valley, Ripollès). One of the capitals supporting the baldachin is from an unknown origin (33 x 29 x 29 cm). Acquisition of the Plandiura Collection, 1932. MNAC/MAC 4523- 4525

82. ALTAR FROM SANT ROMÀ DE VILA. First half of the 13th century. Tempera on wood with stucco relief. 113 x 125 x 91 cm. From the Church of Sant Romà de Vila (Encamp, Andorra). Acquisition, 1922. MNAC/MAC 15875

83. LEAVES OF A DOOR. 12th century (modified in the 18th century.) Wood and wrought iron attached with spherical nails. 220 x 104 cm (MNAC/MAC 39164) and 220 x 79 cm (MNAC/MAC 39165). On permanent loan, 1942. MNAC/MAC 39164, 39165

84. VOUSSOIR FROM RIPOLL. Second half of the 12th century. Stone. 52.5 x 34.5 x 26 cm. From the Monastery of Santa Maria in Ripoll (Ripollès). Gift of Antoni Coll i Fort, 1935. MNAC/MAC 12264

85. CAPITAL. End of the 12th century. Stone. 26 x 23 x 23 cm. Probably from the area of Girona or Empordà. Former collection of the Museo Provincial de Antigüedades in Barcelona. MNAC/MAC 14228

86. FRAGMENT OF A CAPITAL. Second half of the 12th century. Marble. 26 x 30 x 17.5 cm. Probably from Roussillon. On permanent loan, 1984. MNAC/MAC 122501

87. CAPITAL. First third of the 13th century. Marble. 33 x 27 x 21 cm. Acquisition, 1906. MNAC/MAC 24028

88. CAPITALS FROM BESALÚ. Between 1137 and 1167/71. Stone. 66.5 x 69 x 49.5 cm (MNAC/MAC 200685); 64 x 60 x 55 cm (MNAC/MAC 200686); 66.5 x 65 x 36.5 cm (MNAC/MAC 200687); 64 x 56 x 56 cm (MNAC/MAC 200688) and 63 x 56.5 x 56.5 cm (MNAC/MAC 200689). From the Church of Santa Maria in Besalú (Garrotxa). On permanent loan from the Generalitat de Catalunya (Autonomous Government of Catalonia), Gòdia dation, 1994. MNAC/MAC 200685-200689

89. CAPITALS FROM TAVÈRNOLES. Second half of the 12th century. Granite. 38 x 37.5 x 37.5 cm (MNAC/MAC 22994); 37.5 x 39 x 39 cm (MNAC/MAC 22995); 33 x 37 x 29 cm (MNAC/MAC 24005); 39 x 39 x 30 cm (MNAC/MAC 24007) and 38 x 39 x 38 cm (MNAC/MAC 24008). From the cloister of the Monastery of Sant Serni de Tavèrnoles (Les Valls de Valira, Alt Urgell). Acquisition, 1906. MNAC/MAC 22994, 22995, 24005, 24007, 24008

90. FRAGMENTS OF THE CLOISTER OF SANT PERE DE LES PUEL·LES. After 1187. Stone (the traces of polychromy are later.) 210 x 347 x 90 cm. From the old Monastery of Sant Pere de les Puel·les in Barcelona. Former collection of the Museo Provincial de Antigüedades in Barcelona. MNAC/MAC 113143

91. THE SO-CALLED DOUBLE CAPITAL FROM ORPESA. Second half of the 12th century. Stone. 29 x 44 x 25 cm. Acquisition of the Plandiura Collection, 1932. MNAC/MAC 5289

92.1 CAPITALS OF THE PILLAR FROM CAMARASA. First third of the 13th century. Stone. 55 x 47 x 43 cm (MNAC/MAC 17601); 55 x 56 x 59 cm (MNAC/MAC 17602); 55 x 56 x 50 cm (MNAC/MAC 17603); 55 x 45 x 51 cm (MNAC/MAC 17604) and 56 x 56 x 80 cm (MNAC/MAC 17605). From the transept of the Church of Sant Miquel, Camarasa Castle (Noguera). Acquisition, 1929. MNAC/MAC 17601-17605

92.2 CAPITALS FROM THE APSE AT CAMARASA. First third of the 13th century. Stone. 30 x 45 x 26 cm (MNAC/MAC 24010); 34 x 30 x 30 cm (MNAC/MAC 24011); 33 x 52 x 29 cm (MNAC/MAC 24014); 33 x 45 x 31 cm (MNAC/MAC 24020) and 31 x 51 x 32 cm (MNAC/MAC 24021). From the apse of the Church of Sant Miquel, Camarasa Castle (Noguera). Acquisition, 1929. MNAC/MAC 24010, 24011, 24014, 24020, 24021

93. CAPITAL. First half of the 13th century. Stone. 27 x 19 x 19 cm. Probably from Barcelona. Former collection of the Museo Provincial de Antigüedades in Barcelona. MNAC/MAC 15995

94. CAPITALS FROM SANT PERE DE LES PUEL·LES. End of the 12th century. Stone (the traces of polychromy are later). 32.5 x 38.5 x 31.5 cm (MNAC/MAC 9867) and 32 x 35 x 26.5 cm (MNAC/MAC 9868). From a doorway of the Monastery of Sant Pere de les Puel·les in Barcelona. Former collection of the Museo Provincial de Antigüedades in Barcelona. MNAC/MAC 9867, 9868

95. CAPITALS. 12th century. Stone. 32 x 37 x 39 cm (MNAC/MAC 24004) and 42 x 42 x 41 cm (MNAC/MAC 24018). Acquisition, 1906. MNAC/MAC 24004, 24018

96. CAPITALS FROM THE CONVENT OF SANT FRANCESC. *c.* 1200-20. Marble. 28 x 23 x 23.5 cm (MNAC/MAC 14202); 28 x 26 x 23.5 cm (MNAC/MAC 14203) and 30 x 19 x 19 cm (MNAC/MAC 14206). Discovered in Barcelona, on the former site of the Hospital of Sant Nicolau, subsequently the Convent of Sant Francesc. Former collection of the Museo Provincial de Antigüedades in Barcelona. MNAC/MAC 14202, 14203, 14206

97. CAPITAL. First quarter of the 13th century. Marble. 28 x 25 x 24.5 cm. Acquisition of the Plandiura Collection, 1932. MNAC/MAC 5290

98. CAPITAL. Second third of the 12th century. Stone. 32 x 53 x 30 cm. Probably from Languedoc or Gascogne (France). Acquisition, 1907. MNAC/MAC 24109

99. CAPITAL. Reused as holy water stoup. First third of the 13th century. Marble. 26 x 28 x 16 cm. Probably from Tarragona. Former collection of the Museo Provincial de Antigüedades in Barcelona. MNAC/MAC 24017

100. CAPITAL FROM BREDA. Beginning of the 13th century. Stone. 25.5 x 22 x 22 cm. From the cloister of the Monastery of Sant Salvador de Breda (Selva). Former collection of the Museo Provincial de Antigüedades in Barcelona. MNAC/MAC 14097

101. CAPITAL FROM THE CATHEDRAL OF TARRAGONA. Second half of the 13th century. Marble. 34 x 24 x 24 cm. From the Cathedral of Tarragona. Acquisition, 1906. MNAC/MAC 24027

102. PAINTINGS FROM THE CHURCH OF SANTA MARIA IN TAÜLL. The east end paintings from *c.* 1123; the rest of the paintings were done later. Fresco. Central apse: 655 x 370 x 500 cm (MNAC/MAC 15863). From the Church of Santa Maria in Taüll (La Vall de Boí, Alta Ribagorça). Acquisition, 1919-23, 1960 and 1971. MNAC/MAC 15836, 15847, 15856, 15857, 15857b, 15859, 15859b, 15859c, 15861, 15863, 15864, 15958-15961, 15965, 15965b, 63924, 63925, 200413-200417, 200443, 200473

102.1 ALTAR FROM SANTA MARIA IN TAÜLL. *c.* 1123. Fresco. 98 x 175.5 x 99 cm. From the main apse of the Church of Santa Maria in Taüll (La Vall de Boí, Alta Ribagorça). Acquisition, 1960. MNAC/MAC 113141

103. ALTAR FRONTAL FROM SANTA MARIA IN TAÜLL. Second half of the 12th century. Wood carvings with polychromy in tempera, applied to the frontal (repainted in 1579). 135 x 98 cm. From the Church of Santa Maria in Taüll (La Vall de Boí, Alta Ribagorça). Acquisition of the Plandiura Collection, 1932. MNAC/MAC 3904

104. CHRIST FROM SANTA MARIA IN TAÜLL. 12th century (modern cross). Wood carving with traces of polychromy in tempera. 50 x 50 x 12.5 cm. From the Church of Santa Maria in Taüll (La Vall de Boí, Alta Ribagorça). Acquisition of the Plandiura Collection, 1932. MNAC/MAC 3930

105. VIRGIN. *c.* 1200. Wood carving with traces of polychromy in tempera. 72 x 28 x 22 cm. Acquisition of the Plandiura Collection, 1932. MNAC/MAC 3923

106. VIRGIN. First half of the 13th century. Wood carving with traces of polychromy in tempera. 80 x 30 x 22 cm. Probably from Castile. Acquisition of the Plandiura Collection, 1932. MNAC/MAC 3924

107. VIRGIN FROM ALL. *c.* 1200. Wood carving with polychromy in tempera varnished with *colradura*. 88 x 38 x 29 cm. From the Church of Santa Maria in All (Isòvol, Baixa Cerdanya). Acquisition, 1920. MNAC/MAC 15917

108 VIRGIN FROM COVET. 13th century. Wood carving with polychromy in tempera. 83 x 31 x 24 cm. From Santa Maria in Covet (Isona i Conca Dellà, Pallars Jussà). Acquisition of the Plandiura Collection, 1932. MNAC/MAC 4395

109. VIRGIN. 13th century. Wood carving with polychromy in tempera. 85 x 23 x 16 cm. Acquisition, 1950. MNAC/MAC 35740

110. VIRGIN OF THE DURRO DESCENT FROM THE CROSS. 12th century. Wood carving with traces of polychromy in tempera. 189 x 51 x 23 cm. From the Church of the Nativitat de Maria in Durro (La Vall de Boí, Alta Ribagorça). Acquisition, 1922. MNAC/MAC 15895

111. VIRGIN AND ST. JOHN OF THE ERILL-LA-VALL DESCENT FROM THE CROSS. 12th century. Wood carvings with traces of polychromy in tempera. 144 x 40 x 21 cm (each one). From the Church of Santa Eulàlia in Erill-la-Vall (La Vall de Boí, Alta Ribagorça). Acquisition of the Plandiura Collection, 1932. MNAC/MAC 3917, 3918

112. FIGURES OF THE SANTA MARIA IN TAÜLL DESCENT FROM THE CROSS. 12th or 13th century. Wood carvings with traces of polychromy in tempera. Christ: 122 x 168 x 22 cm; Joseph of Arimathea: 103 x 38 x 29 cm; Virgin: 110 x 29 x 17 cm; Dymas: 100 x 20 x 15 cm. From the Church of Santa Maria in Taüll (La Vall de Boí, Alta Ribagorça). Acquisition of the Plandiura Collection, 1932. MNAC/MAC 3915

113. THE CHRIST FROM 1147. Consecrated in the year 1147 (according to a parchment found in the rear of the piece). Wood carving (restored in the 17th century). Christ: 100 x 91 x 16 cm; cross: 187 x 118 x 4.5 cm. From the bishopric of Urgell. Acquisition, 1906. MNAC/MAC 15950

114. THE BATLLÓ MAJESTY. Middle of the 12th century. Wood carving with traces of polychromy in tempera. Christ: 94 x 96 x 17 cm; cross 156 x 120 x 4 cm. From Garrotxa. Gift of Enric Batlló, 1914. MNAC/MAC 15937

115. PAINTINGS FROM SORPE. Middle of the 12th century. Fresco. 670 x 664 x 896 cm. From the Church of Sant Pere in Sorpe (Alt Àneu, Àneu Valley, Pallars Sobirà). Acquisition, 1946 and 1964. MNAC/MAC 113144

116. ALTAR FRONTAL FROM DURRO. 12th century. Tempera on wood. 100 x 120 cm. From the Hermitage of Sant Quirze i Santa Julita in Durro (La Vall de Boí, Alta Ribagorça). Acquisition, 1923. MNAC/MAC 15809

117. APSE FROM ESTAON. Second half of the 12th century. Fresco. 480 x 435 x 250 cm. From the Church of Santa Eulàlia in Estaon (Cardós Valley, Pallars Sobirà). Acquisition, 1919-1923. MNAC/MAC 15969

118. ST. JOHN OF SURP. Second third of the 12th century. Fresco. 128 x 52 cm. From the apse of the Church of Sant Iscle i Santa Victòria in Surp (Rialb de Noguera, Pallars Sobirà). Acquisition, 1963. MNAC/MAC 69492

119. PAINTINGS FROM SANT ROMÀ IN LES BONS. *c.* 1164. Fresco. The twelve Apostles and Mary: 166 x 342 cm (MNAC/MAC 15783); Christ in Majesty: 103 x 272 cm (MNAC/MAC 15787). From the apse of Sant Romà in Les Bons (Encamp, Andorra). Gift of Lluís Plandiura, 1932. MNAC/MAC 15783, 15787

120. APSE FROM ENGOLASTERS. *c.* 1160. Fresco. 360 x 305 x 195 cm. From the Church of Sant Miquel in Engolasters (Les Escaldes, Andorra). Acquisition, 1919-23. MNAC/MAC 15972

121. PAINTINGS FROM SANT ESTEVE IN ANDORRA LA VELLA. *c.* 1200-10. Fresco. Apsidiole: 255 x 185 x 85 cm (MNAC/MAC 35711); Luke's winged ox: 97 x 198 cm (MNAC/MAC 35706); Christ: 95 x 64 cm (MNAC/MAC 35707); architectural frieze: 55 x 156 cm (MNAC/MAC 35708); plant border: 41 x 463 cm (MNAC/MAC 35709, 35710). From the Church of Sant Esteve in Andorra la Vella (Andorra). Acquisition, 1950. MNAC/MAC 35706-35711

122. ALTAR FRONTAL FROM AVIÀ. *c.* 1170-90. Tempera on wood with stucco relief varnished with *colradura*. 105 x 176 cm. From the Church of Santa Maria in Avià (Berguedà). Acquisition, 1903. MNAC/MAC 15784

123. ALTAR FRONTAL FROM BALTARGA. *c.* 1200. Tempera on wood. 94 x 165 cm. From the Church of Sant Andreu in Baltarga (Bellver de Cerdanya, Baixa Cerdanya). Acquisition, 1911. MNAC/MAC 15804

124. THE TAVÈRNOLES BALDACHIN. First half of the 13th century. Tempera on wood with stucco relief. 170 x 216 cm. From the Monastery of Sant Serni de Tavèrnoles (Les Valls de Valira, Alt Urgell). Acquisition, 1906. MNAC/MAC 24060

125. THE PASSION BEAM. *c.* 1200-20. Tempera on wood. 20.5 x 230.5 cm. Acquisition, 1907. MNAC/MAC 15833

126. THE CARDET BEAM. Middle of the 13th century. Tempera on wood. 22 x 390 cm. From the Church of Santa Maria in Cardet (La Vall de Boí, Alta Ribagorça). Acquisition, 1962. MNAC/MAC 71999

127. ATRIUM FROM CARDONA. *c.* 1200. Fresco. 475 x 860 x 523 cm. From the Church of Sant Vicenç in Cardona (Bages). On permanent loan, 1953. MNAC/MAC 200715

128. CENSER. *c.* 1220-50. Openwork on engraved cast copper. 13 x 12 cm (diameter). Gift of Enric Batlló, 1914. MNAC/MAC 12118

129. CENSER. 13th century. Openwork on engraved cast copper. 13.5 x 11 cm (diameter). Former collection of the Museo Provincial de Antigüedades in Barcelona. MNAC/MAC 9491

130. CENSER. Limoges, second half of the 13th century. *Champlevé* enamelling on gilded openwork cast copper. 13.5 x 11 cm (diameter). Bequest of Santiago Espona, 1958. MNAC/MAC 65548

131. CENSER. Limoges, second half of the 13th century. *Champlevé* enamelling on engraved and gilded openwork cast copper. 18.5 x 14 cm (diameter). Acquisition of the Plandiura Collection, 1932. MNAC/MAC 4550

132. INCENSE BOAT FROM ARS. Limoges, second half of the 13th century. *Champlevé* enamelling and cabuchons on engraved openwork cast copper. 3 x 15 x 85 cm. From the church in Ars (Les Valls de Valira, Alt Urgell). Acquisition, 1906. MNAC/MAC 12093

133. EUCHARISTIC DOVE. Limoges, first half of the 13th century. *Champlevé* enamelling on gilded cast copper. 18 x 21 x 7.3 cm (diameter of lower disc). Bequest of Santiago Espona, 1958. MNAC/MAC 65534

134. THE MONDOÑEDO CROZIER. Limoges, *c.* 1200. *Champlevé* enamelling on gilded engraved cast copper with cast figures in full relief. Volute diameter: 32 x 15 cm; knob diameter: 8 cm. From a sarcophagus said to have housed the body of the Bishop of Ribadeo, Pelayo de Cebeyra (Siveira) (1199-1218). Placed in the Cathedral of Mondoñedo *c.* 1855 (Lugo). Acquisition of the Plandiura Collection, 1932. MNAC/MAC 4544

135. CIBORIUM FROM CERDANYA. Limoges, *c.* 1195-1200. *Champlevé* enamelling on gilded and engraved cast copper. 13.5 x 14 cm (diameter). From a church in Cerdanya. Acquisition, 1918. MNAC/MAC 12106

136. CHRIST. *c.* 1180. Engraved gilded and cast bronze. 20 x 13.3 x 3.7 cm. Acquisition of the Plandiura Collection, 1932. MNAC/MAC 4552

137. RELIQUARY CASKET. The Holy Innocents. Limoges, *c.* 1200-10. *Champlevé* enamelling on gilded cast copper over a wood core and heads in relief. 17.5 x 19.5 x 7.4 cm. Bequest of Santiago Espona, 1958. MNAC/MAC 65529

138. CHÂSSE. Limoges, *c.* 1250. *Champlevé* enamelling, figures and encrusted gems on gilded cast copper over a wood core. 27.5 x 22.5 x 9.3 cm. Bequest of Santiago Espona, 1958. MNAC/MAC 65527

139. CHÂSSE. Limoges, *c.* 1210-20. *Champlevé* enamelling on gilded cast copper. Cast heads. 21 x 18 x 8.5 cm. Acquisition of the Plandiura Collection, 1932. MNAC/MAC 4573

140. CHRIST ON THE CROSS. Limoges, second half of the 13th century. Cast and gilded copper over a wood core with applied figures and plaques in *champlevé* enamel plus encrusted cabochons. 46.4 x 25.5 x 3.3 cm. Acquisition, 1914. MNAC/MAC 12110

141. APSE FROM TOSES. 13th century. Fresco. 496 x 385 x 140 cm. From the Church of Sant Cristòfol in Toses (Ribes Valley, Ripollès). Acquisition, 1952. MNAC/MAC 47474

141.1 BEAM FROM THE APSE OF TOSES. 13th century. Tempera on wood. 18 x 14 x 325 cm. From the Church of Sant Cristòfol in Toses (Ribes Valley, Ripollès). Acquisition, 1952. MNAC/MAC 47475

142. ALTAR FRONTAL OF THE ARCHANGELS. *c.* 1220-50. Tempera on wood with stucco relief varnished with *colradura*. 106 x 127 cm. Acquisition of the Plandiura Collection, 1932. MNAC/MAC 3913

143. SIDE PANELS FROM THE ALTAR OF ORÓS. First half of the 13th century. Tempera on wood. 80 x 80 cm (each one). From the Church of Sant Pere in Orós (La Guingueta d'Àneu, Pallars Sobirà). Acquisition of the Plandiura Collection, 1932. MNAC/MAC 3906, 3907

144. ALTAR FRONTAL FROM FARRERA DE PALLARS. Middle of the 13th century. Tempera on wood. 103 x 147 cm. Probably from the original Church in Farrera de Pallars (Ferrera Valley, Pallars Sobirà). Acquisition, 1911. MNAC/MAC 15808

145. ST. CATHERINE OF ISAVARRE. Second half of the 13th century. Fresco. 96 x 61 cm. From the apse of the Church of Sant Llorenç in Isavarre (Alt Àneu, Àneu Valley, Pallars Sobirà). Acquisition, 1963. MNAC/MAC 69507

146. ROYAL COINAGE

146.1 Alfons I the Chaste, *Diner de quatern* (1162-96), minted in Barcelona. Billon. 0.78 g, 19 mm. MNAC/GNC 109233

146.2 Alfons I the Chaste, *Diner* (1162-96), minted in Marseilles. Billon. 0.86 g, 18 mm. MNAC/GNC 12906

146.3 James I the Conqueror, *Diner de doblenc* (1213-76), minted in Barcelona. Billon. 0.91 g, 17 mm. MNAC/GNC 27857

146.4 and 146.5 James I the Conqueror, *Diner de tern* (1213-76), minted in Barcelona. Billon. 0.89 g, 18 mm. (MNAC/GNC 34121) y 1.01 g, 18 mm. (MNAC/GNC 15297)

146.6 James I the Conqueror, *Diner de tern* (1213-76), minted in Aragon. Billon. 0.83 g, 18 mm. MNAC/GNC 33351

146.7 James I the Conqueror, *Diner de tern* (1213-76), minted in Valencia. Billon. 1.21 g, 17 mm. MNAC/GNC 100064

146.8 *Diner melgorés* from the seigneury of Montpellier. 13th century. Billon. 1.02 g, 17 mm. MNAC/GNC 35162

147. ALTAR FRONTAL FROM CHÍA. Signed by John (IOH[ANNE]S PINTOR ME FECIT). Second half of the 13th century. Tempera on wood with stucco relief formerly varnished with *colradura*. 99 x 145 cm. From the Church of San Martín in Chía (Benasque Valley, Huesca). Acquisition of the Plandiura Collection, 1932. MNAC/MAC 3902

148. ALTAR FRONTAL FROM RIGATELL. Second half of the 13th century. Tempera on wood with stucco relief formerly varnished with *colradura*. 104.6 x 112 cm. From the Sanctuary of the Virgin de Rigatell (Areny de Noguera/Arén, Huesca). Guift of Julio Muñoz, 1950. MNAC/MAC 35701

149. ALTAR FRONTAL FROM SANT PERE IN BOÍ. Second half of the 13th century. Tempera on wood with stucco relief formerly varnished with *colradura*. 88 x 158 cm. From the former Chapel of Sant Pere in Boí (La Vall de Boí, Alta Ribagorça). Acquisition of the Plandiura Collection, 1932. MNAC/MAC 3912

150. CROSS. Second half of the 13th century. Tempera on wood with stucco relief formerly varnished with *colradura*. 120 x 56 cm. From the former collection of the Barcelona Museums. MNAC/MAC 17625

151. PAINTINGS FROM SAN PEDRO IN ARLANZA. *c.* 1210. Fresco. Griffin: 190 x 320 cm (MNAC/MAC 40142); castle: 139 x 189 cm (MNAC/MAC 40144); mythical animal: 106 x 84 cm (MNAC/MAC 40145). From a chamber in the Torre del Tesoro in the Monastery of San Pedro in Arlanza (Burgos). Acquisition, 1943. MNAC/MAC 40142, 40144, 40145

152. CHAPTER HOUSE FROM SANTA MARÍA IN SIGENA. *c.* 1190-94. Fresco. From the Nunnery of Santa María in Sigena (Villanueva de Sigena, Huesca). Admission, 1940. MNAC/MAC 68703-68709

153. PYX. Limoges, last quarter of the 13th century. *Champlevé* enamelling on gilded cast copper. 11 x 8.5 cm. Acquisition of the Plandiura Collection, 1932. MNAC/MAC 4590

Glossary

ABACUS
In architecture, upper part of the capital on which the impost or the components of the arch or the vault are located.

ALTAR STONE
Consecrated stone on which the Eucharist is celebrated.

AMBULATORY
In architecture, aisle or nave running around the east end of a church.

APOCRYPHA, BOOKS OR GOSPELS
Jewish and Christian texts which given their titles and content are related to the books of the Bible, but have not been recognized by the Catholic Church.

ATRIUM
Porticoed enclosure in a church which precedes the main entrance and is set at right angles to the naves. Also called a narthex.

BEATUS
Name by which the *Commentaries on the Book of Revelation* is known. It was written in the 8th century by Beatus, a monk from Liébana. There are numerous copies of this text, many of them illustrated. They were produced in the Middle Ages and today they are very valuable codices for the history of the arts of colour during this period.

BELL
Main body of the capital between the abacus and the astragal or necking. This word comes from the shape it has in the Corinthian capital; it is also called the vase or basket.

BESTIARY
Natural history treatise on real or imaginary animals with an allegorical meaning. In the medieval world, it referred to zoömorphic representations that often took on a symbolic or moralizing import.

BEVELLING
In sculpture, a way of cutting obliquely into the external face of an object or surface. Bevelling is used especially for geometric and floral motifs.

CABOCHON
Any stone, precious or not, encrusted in a gold or silver object.

CARMINA
Latin term for a collection of medieval liturgical chants and poems.

CHAMPLEVÉ
Enamelling technique that consists of making cavities in metal sheeting and filling them with glass paste.

CHISEL
Long flat steel tool which has its cutting edge on the end. It is used in sculpture to cut stone.

CLIPEUS
In Christian art, a circular medallion on which an image or a sign was inscribed. The word comes from Roman times when shields had a circular shape and sometimes also had the bust of a god or a personage engraved on it.

CLOISONNÉ
Enamelling technique that consists of placing glass paste in small cells formed by thin metallic strips placed perpendicularly on the surface of the sheet-metal to be decorated.

CORINTHIAN
One of the classical architectural orders characterized by capitals with two rows of acanthus leaves, volutes at the corner, and a rosette on the upper central part.

CROZIER
Staff or crook that bishops or abbots carry as a symbol of their authority. In the Romanesque period it offen has an ornamental top curved in the shape of a scroll.

CUFIC SCRIPT
Variety of Arabic script characterized by rigid and angular flourishes. This typology appears, for example, in Caliphal capitals.

EMBOSSING
Technique used in precious metalwork and in other arts involving metal for obtaining work in relief. It consists of hammering the inner side of the metal sheet intended for decoration.

EPIPHANY
The Adoration of the Magi, or the Adoration of Jesus by the Three Kings, one of the most solemn feast days of the Christian liturgical year and by extension, the depiction of this episode in the New Testament, which is understood as the first manifestation of the divinity of Christ.

EPITAPHIOS THRENOS
Lamentation over the dead Christ. It was originally a Byzantine iconographic theme in which Christ, after being taken from the cross, is placed by Nicodemus and Joseph of Arimathea on the unction stone, prior to His entombment. The Virgin, St. John the Evangelist and Mary Magdalene appear weeping in depictions of this theme.

ETIMASIA
Iconographic depiction of the empty throne of Christ, made ready for Him to occupy it on the Day of the Last Judgement.

FRESCO
Mural technique that consists of applying pigments on a lime plaster surface while it is still fresh, that is, damp.

FRET
Geometric ornamental border made up of a continous right-angled line which constantly repeats the same design.

FRIEZE
Decorative element which unfolds horizontally. It comes from the horizontal space which, in classical architecture, is found between the architrave and the cornice.

GRIFFIN
Mythological hybrid being of ancient origin which has the head and the wings of an eagle and the body of a lion. It appears in pictorial and sculptural representations in medieval art.

HEGIRA
Name given to Muhammad's flight from Mecca to the future Medina in 622 A.D. The dating of the years in the Muslin calendar begins from this date.

ICONOGRAPHY
Subsidiary science of art history which concerns the identification, description, classification and interpretation of the arts. It also involves their sources and the codificaction and development of themes and subject matter.

IMPOST
Block of stone, with or without mouldings, on which an arch or vault rests.

INTRADOS
Interior surface of an arch or vault.

LINTEL
Horizontal stone which closes the upper part of a door or window, and whose ends rest on the jambs.

LITANY
Prayer consisting of alternating responses and made up of a more or less long series of invocations and supplications.

MAIESTAS DOMINI
The Lord in All His Majesty. Depiction of Christ enthroned within a mandorla. His right hand is in a gesture of blessing and His left hand often holds the Book of Life. He is usually accompanied by the Tetramorph, angels and archangels, and at times by the twenty-four Elders of the Apocalypse (see **Theophany**).

MAIESTAS MARIAE
Representation of Mary enthroned with the Holy Child on her lap, within the mandorla as *sedes sapientiae* or the Seat of Wisdom.

MANDORLA
Aureola where the figure of the *Maiestas Domini*, as a sign of divinity, or the *Maiestas Mariae* is inscribed. Also called the **mystical almond**.

MITRE
Item of clothing for covering the heads of bishops and abbots, and used during liturgical rites as a symbol of their power.

MYSTICAL ALMOND
See **Mandorla**

NECKING
In architecture, a moulding of ring between the capital and the shaft of a column. In the classical world it is found in the upper part of the shaft, and in the Romanesque it is usually part of the capital. It is sometimes called the astragal.

PANTOCRATOR
The Almighty, an epithet for God and the three persons of the Trinity individually. The word designates the most common image of Christ, in which He is frontally depicted giving the blessing with His right hand and holding the book in His left. On Byzantine domes there is often a bust of the Pantocrator Christ.

PAROUSIA
Appearance of the divinity, coming of Christ. The Second Parousia refers to His coming at the end of time.

PASSIO
Account of the death of a martyr and the events that led up to this.

PHYLACTERY
Ribbon with a legend or inscription on it, worn by certain saints in iconographic representations.

PSYCHOSTASIS
Weighing of the deeds of souls by the Archangel St. Michael, an episode that forms part of the Last Judgement.

SEDES SAPIENTIAE
Seat of Wisdom, a term applied to the Virgin as a throne for the Holy Child.

SERAPHIM
Angel which, like the cherubim, belongs to the highest angelic hierarchy. In Romanesque art, it is depicted with three pairs of wings, two of which are replete with eyes.

SHAFT
Trunk of a column located between the capital and the base.

STACCO
Technique for removing frescoes from a wall. It consists of removing the pictorial layer along with the layer of lime plaster or mortar.

STRAPPO
Technique for removing frescoes from a wall. It consists of removing only the pictorial layer, without the mortar.

STUCCO
Lime or plaster mortar which was applied on certain frontals to obtain figures in relief, borders or moulded backgrounds which were subsequently painted or gilded. There are also other modalities of stucco like, for example, the kind used as a wall facing which, given its fragility, has more often than not disappeared.

SYNOPTIC GOSPELS
Term designating the Gospels of Matthew, Mark and Luke which, since they have remarkable similarity, give us an overall vision of their mutual agreement.

TEMPERA
Pictorial technique in which the pigments are mixed with non-oil-based agglutinating agents.

TETRAMORPH
The four symbols of the Evangelists: the angel for Matthew, the eagle for John, the ox for Luke and the lion for Mark.

THEOPHANY
Manifestation of divinity. In Romanesque art, it is usually found on apse vaulting. It is the manifestation of the Lord in All His Majesty (*Maiestas Domini*), accompanied by the Tetramorph, angels and archangels. In that instance the literary source is the Book of Revelation, plus elements taken from the visions of the prophets Isaiah and Ezekiel and the Book of Daniel.

THURIFER ANGEL
Angel which carries the censer.

TREPANNING
Procedure applied to sculpture which consists of drilling holes in the stone.

TYMPANUM
Surface situated between the lintel of a door and the arch above it. In the Romanesque period, it usually had a semicircular shape. In general, it can also be the interior space of a pediment whether it is triangular or curvilinear.

VERMICULATION
Decoration using plant forms of a sinnous kind, used in precious metalwork and work in copper which is found, for example, alongside enamelling. It should not be confused with the mosaic technique, the *opus vermiculatum* used in classical Antiquity.

VOUSSOIR
Each of the stone blocks that form an arch.

VOLUTE
Ornament in the shape of a spiral, characteristic of Ionic capitals, but also found on Corinthian and composite capitals. It appears in this way on medieval capitals, the composition of which frequently derives from Antiquity.

Bibliography

NOTE: The titles in this bibliography —necessarily restricted— have been chosen because they are considered among the most outstanding books and articles written on the subject, or they are recent publications, more easily available to readers and just as valuable. Although they have not been included here, there are other internationally known authors who should not be forgotten, for example: Kuhn, Porter, Grabar, Demus and others, all of whom have contributed to the study of Romanesque art in Catalonia.

GENERAL

AINAUD DE LASARTE, J., *La peinture romane*, Paris, 1963.

AINAUD DE LASARTE, J., *La pintura catalana. La fascinació del romànic*, Geneva-Barcelona, 1989.

AINAUD DE LASARTE, J., *Catalogne romane*, La pierre-qui-Vire, Zodiaque, 1994.

L'art català, Barcelona, 1957 (directed by J. Folch i Torres).

BARRAL I ALTET, X., *L'art pre-romànic a Catalunya. Segles IX-X*, Barcelona, 1981.

BASTARDES, R., *Les talles romàniques del Sant Crist a Catalunya*, Barcelona, 1978.

BORRÀS GUALIS, G.M.; GARCÍA GUATAS, M., *La pintura románica en Aragón*, Zaragoza, 1978.

BOTET I SISÓ, J., *Les monedes catalanes*, 3 vols., Barcelona, 1908-11.

CARBONELL I ESTELLER, E., *L'Art Romànic a Catalunya. Segle XII*, 2 vols., Barcelona, 1974-75.

CARBONELL I ESTELLER, E., *L'ornamentació en la pintura romànica catalana*, Barcelona, 1981.

Catalunya Medieval, Barcelona, 1992 (Exhibition Catalogue).

Catalunya Romànica, 27 vols., Barcelona, Fundació Enciclopèdia Catalana, 1984-98.

COOK, W.W.S., 'The earliest painted panels of Catalonia' in *The Art Bulletin*, New York, V, no. 4, 1922, pp. 85-101; VI, no. 2, 1923, pp. 31-60; VIII, no. 2, 1926, pp. 57-104; VIII, no. 4, 1926, pp. 195-234; X, no. 2, 1927, pp. 153-204; X, no. 4, 1928, pp. 305-365.

COOK, W.W.S.; GUDIOL RICART, J., *Pintura e imaginería románicas*, Madrid, 1950 (Ars Hispaniae, VI) (2nd edition revised by J. Gudiol, Madrid, 1980).

CRUSAFONT I SABATER, M., *Numismática de la Corona catalano-aragonesa medieval* (785-1516), Madrid, 1982.

DALMASES, N. DE; JOSÉ I PITARCH, A., *L'època del Cister s. XIII*, Barcelona, 1985 (Història de l'art català, II).

DALMASES, N. DE; JOSÉ I PITARCH, A., *Els inicis i l'art romànic s. IX-XII*, Barcelona, 1986 (Història de l'art català, I).

DURLIAT, M., *Roussillon roman*, La Pierre-qui-Vire, Zodiaque, 1958 (revised Spanish edition, Madrid, 1988).

DURLIAT, M., *Art Catalan*, Paris-Grenoble, 1963.

DURLIAT, M., *Art roman*, Paris, 1982.

FOLCH I TORRES, J., *La pintura romànica sobre fusta*, Barcelona, 1956 (Monumenta Cataloniae, IX).

GAUTHIER, M. M., *L'époque romane. Émaux méridionaux. Catalogue Internationale de l'Oeuvre de Limoges*, Paris, 1987.

GUDIOL I CUNILL, J., *La pintura mig-eval catalana. Els Primitius*, 2 vols., Barcelona, 1927.

GUDIOL RICART, J.; GAYA NUÑO, J. A., *Aquitectura y escultura románicas*, Madrid, 1948 (Ars Hispaniae, V).

JUNYENT, E., *Catalogne romane*, 2 vols., La Pierre-qui-Vire, Zodiaque, 1960-61

MATAS I BLANXART, M.T., *Els esmalts romànics a Catalunya. 1. Arquetes*, Barcelona, 1982.

Millenum. Història i art de l'Església catalana, Barcelona, 1989 (Exhibition Catalogue).

PIJOAN, J., *Les pintures murals catalanes*, 4 parts, Barcelona, Institut d'Estudis Catalans, 1907-21.

PIJOAN, J.; GUDIOL, J., *Les pintures murals romàniques de Catalunya*, Barcelona, 1948 (Monumenta Cataloniae, VI).

POST, CH. R., *A History of Spanish painting*, 14 vols., Cambridge (Mass.), Harvard University Press, 1930-66.

PUIG I CADAFALCH, J., *L'escultura romànica a Catalunya*, 3 vols., Barcelona, 1949-54 (Monumenta Cataloniae, V-VII).

SUREDA, J., *La pintura romànica a Catalunya*, Madrid, 1982.

SUREDA, J., *La pintura románica en España (Aragón, Navarra, Castilla-León y Galicia)*, Madrid, 1985.

The Art of Medieval Spain. A. D. 500-1200, New York, The Metropolitan Museum of Art, 1993 (Exhibition Catalogue).

Thesaurus/Estudis. L'art als bisbats de Catalunya. 1000-1800, Barcelona, 1986 (Exhibition Catalogue).

TRENS, M., *Les Majestats catalanes*, Barcelona, 1966 (Monumenta Cataloniae, XIII).

YARZA, J., *Arte y arquitectura en España. 500-1250*, Madrid, 1979.

THE MUSEUM GUIDES AND CATALOGUES

1888
ELÍAS DE MOLINS, A., *Catálogo del Museo Provincial de Antigüedades de Barcelona*, Barcelona.

1906
Catálogo del Museo de Bellas Artes de Barcelona, Barcelona.

1926
FOLCH I TORRES, J., *Museo de la Ciudadela. Catálogo de la sección de arte románico*, Barcelona.

1936
Junta de Museus. Catàleg del Museu d'Art de Catalunya. Primera part, Barcelona.

1937
L'art catalan du Xe *au XV*[e] *siècle*, Paris.
L'art catalan à Paris, Paris.

1961
L'Art Roman. Exposición organizada por el Gobierno Español bajo los auspicios del Consejo de Europa. Catálogo, Barcelona, Santiago de Compostela (French edition, Barcelona, 1961).

1973
AINAUD DE LASARTE, J., *Art Romànic. Guia*, Barcelona.

1988
L'època de les catedrals. Romànic/Gòtic. Tresors del Museu d'Art de Catalunya, Girona.

1989
Entorn a Jaume I. De l'art romànic a l'art gòtic, Valencia.

1990
Capolavori dal Museo d'Arte della Catalogna, Rome.

1992
Prefiguració del Museu Nacional d'Art de Catalunya, Barcelona.

1993
GUARDIA, M.; CAMPS, J.; LORÉS, I., *La descoberta de la pintura romànica catalana*, Barcelona.

1995
Agnus Dei. L'art romànic i els artistes del segle XX, Barcelona.

THE MUSEUM PERIODICAL EDITIONS

Butlletí dels Museus d'Art de Barcelona, Barcelona, I-VII, 1931-37.

Anales y Boletín de los Museos de Arte de Barcelona, Barcelona, I-XVIII, 1941-68.

Butlletí del Museu Nacional d'Art de Catalunya, Barcelona, I-II, 1993-96.

List of contents